PETWORTH MANOR
IN THE
SEVENTEENTH CENTURY

PETWORTH MANOR

IN THE

SEVENTEENTH CENTURY

BY

LORD LECONFIELD

GEOFFREY CUMBERLEGE

OXFORD UNIVERSITY PRESS

London New York Toronto

1954

Oxford University Press, Amen House, London E.C.4
GLASGOW NEW YORK TORONTO MELBOURNE WELLINGTON
BOMBAY CALCUTTA MADRAS KARACHI CAPE TOWN IBADAN
Geoffrey Cumberlege, Publisher to the University

PRINTED IN GREAT BRITAIN

CONTENTS

ILLUSTRATIONS

MAPS

at end of text

INTRODUCTION

THIS book attempts to give some account of manorial life in England in the seventeenth century. The material is taken almost entirely from the records in the muniment room of Petworth House, a large collection dating from Edward III and complete from the beginning of the seventeenth century until the passing of the Birkenhead Act in the twentieth. There is also a huge map of the manor as it was in 1610 prepared by Ralph Treswell, junior, showing every field, close, and croft with its measurement and the name of the tenant. An accompanying terrier gives other details. These are most valuable foundations for any history, despite their many differences in details. The maps at the end of the book have been drawn from them. These maps do not cover the whole area of the manor. A portion lying to the south of maps X and XI and west of map XII, and a small part adjacent to Byworth to the south of map XVII have been omitted as no reference is made to them in the text.[1] The maps have been drawn by Mr. K. C. Jordan, F.R.G.S., and I express my gratitude to him. Unfortunately both map and terrier are sadly uninformative on the town of Petworth.

No attempt has been made, nor does one seem either necessary or desirable, to standardize the names of persons and places. The different versions that occur are collected in the Index. Moreover, they are generally easily recognizable.

L.

1953

[1] See the key-map XVIII.

I

THE MANOR

(1)

THE seventeenth century may be called the golden age of the Manor of Petworth. Previously attainders of its hereditary lords during three periods: from December 1406 to March 1416, from November 1461 to March 1470, and from 1537 to 1557 had broken the continuity of its history. The same fate befell it, but only temporarily, when the 7th Earl of Northumberland was beheaded at York in August 1572. His brother then succeeded to the title as 8th Earl under the remainder clause of the restoration in 1557. But he was not summoned to the House of Lords until 1576. In the meantime he was ordered to reside at Petworth, and manorial accounts for the years 1572–6 are preserved there. After his death in the Tower in 1585 his son succeeded to both estates and title without hindrance. But he in turn narrowly escaped losing them, together with his head, for alleged complicity in the Gunpowder Plot. Instead he was condemned to sixteen years, 1604–20, in the Tower and to a fine of £30,000. A forfeited manor tended to become merely a source of revenue to the Crown. The 8th and 9th Earls were active developers.

The original Honour of Petworth included the manors of Petworth, Sutton, Duncton, Heyshott, Cocking, Barlavington, Stedham, Bignor, and Burton. The Percy Honour of Petworth contained only the manors of Petworth, Sutton, Duncton, and Heyshott. Inquisitions post mortem of 35 Henry III, 8 Edward II, and 26 Edward III confirm this. The last one was of Henry, 11th

Baron Percy whose grandson was created first Percy, Earl of Northumberland. It describes him as having held these four manors of Richard, Earl of Arundel by the service of 22 knights' fees.[1] He was not then a tenant in chief of them. Moreover, Heyshott ceased to be of the Honour in 1536 after the 6th Earl had sold it for £800 to William Fitzwilliam Earl of Southampton, to hold of the King as of the Honour of Petworth, when he bequeathed his estates to the Crown. Thereafter Heyshott remained separated from the Honour until 1761 when Charles, Earl of Egremont recovered it for £5,530.

In the seventeenth century each separate manorial court of the Honour combined the functions of the Court Baron of the freehold tenants in which they were the judges, the Customary Court of the Copyhold tenants with the lord or his steward as the judge, the Court Leet with jurisdiction over petty offences, and the View of Frank Pledge. This was obsolete in the Honour, although a constable was occasionally appointed in the small Rectory Manor. The Rector, as Leland observes, had 'much privelege there concerning certain tenants' living in the town or its immediate neighbourhood. The Duke of Somerset put an end to this empire within an empire when he secured an Act of Parliament constituting Duncton and Northchapel separate parishes from Petworth; and, after the death of the Rev. Edward Pelling, Rector from 1691 until 1718, the lordship was combined with that of Petworth Manor.

Each manor remitted the revenues collected in it to a central Receiver who entered them in the account rolls of the Honour of Petworth. After the accession of Charles I the proceedings of the Petworth manorial Court were recorded also in books, and twenty-five volumes cover the three centuries from 1625 until the passing of the Birken-

[1] This Inquisition is printed in E. B. de Fonblanque, *Annals of the House of Percy*, i. 492–501.

head Act in 1922. The rolls and later the books were the registers of all the ordinances, duties, customs, and conveyances that concerned the lord and his copyhold tenants.[1] All transfers of copyholds had to be presented to the court as surrenders and admittances, so also had deaths of tenants and admissions of heirs to be presented and recorded on the rolls or in the books. From these were written the copies of court roll that were the copyholders' title deeds. The deaths of freehold tenants and the reliefs paid by their heirs were recorded separately. In the first book presentments of the deaths of two freeholders were entered by mistake, but the entries were erased.

The court of the manor of Petworth met with commendable but not absolute regularity on Tuesdays from three weeks to three weeks. One interruption lasted from 5 December 1643 until 14 May 1644. It followed a raid by Cavaliers who drove away 'twenty brave horses' from the 10th Earl's stud to the King's headquarters at Oxford. Writing from Petworth on 4 November 1643, Elizabeth, Countess of Northumberland, the 10th Earl's second wife, painted a gloomy picture of the situation after the Cavaliers had gone:[2]

> Misfortunes are soe general that they ought not to be taken notice of unless wee could mend their condition which made me not trouble you with a relation of they cavaliers.

A general or capital court was summoned every Michaelmas at the end of the manorial year. This was the most important court and every tenant, whether free or customary, who owed suit was expected to attend unless excused. A tenant in default was liable to be amerced according to his social status at rates varying from time to time. Knights and Esquires were fined from 1*s.* to 2*s.* 6*d.*, Gentlemen from 6*d.* to 1*s.* 6*d.*, and freeholders from 3*d.*

[1] A note in a book reads: The rolls being wanting the following abstracts are taken from the Court Books.

[2] *Sussex Archaeological Collections*, xxviii. 98–99.

to *6d.* Only copyholders remained unchanged until early in the eighteenth century, although among them were many prominent farmers. On an average 33 copyholders out of a total of 155 to 160 defaulted annually on their suit to the capital court. To them should be added the freehold defaulters and all who had been excused attendance. Faced with these unsatisfactory returns the court issued an order in 1653:

> That in any case any of the tenants shall fail in not appearing according to the tenure in performing their respective suits of court at any Head Court to be holden for this Honour of Petworth, then the amercements shall be doubled in case the tenants so failing in their appearance have not some reasonable cause that hinders such appearance.

This was an empty threat; and not until 1658 were Knights and Esquires raised from 1*s.* to 1*s.* *6d.* and to 2*s.* *6d.* in 1668, the Gentlemen from *6d.* to 8*d.* and to 1*s.* in 1668, and the freeholders from 3*d.* to *6d.* The copyholders escaped. And the old rates were restored in 1684. The Knights, however, were raised to 2*s.* in 1685. And so the fines remained until the end of the century.

As the court sat at Petworth tenants living in or near it could most conveniently attend. This obvious circumstance is demonstrated by the number of copyholders who were present at fourteen or more of the seventeen or eighteen annual courts and those among them who never missed one.

	Petworth		*Tillington and Upperton*		*Northchapel*	
	14 to 18	*18*	*14 to 18*	*18*	*14 to 18*	*18*
1633/4. .	14	6	4	1	..	..
1641/2. .	28	5	7	..	1	..
1654/5. .	24	15	10	1	1	1

In 1654/5 the copyhold population of the manor was 163,

of whom 67 were classed as of Petworth, 48 of Tillington and Upperton, and 48 of Northchapel. Therefore 34–35 per cent. of Petworth copyholders were present at 14 or more of the courts, 21 per cent. of Tillington, and only 2 per cent. of Northchapel. More significant are the numbers of those who did not miss a court: as, for example, the Petworth fifteen who earned this distinction in 1654/5. On one the court rolls give no information. Of the fourteen others only one came from outside the town. Another was represented by the steward of the manor. The remaining twelve were town dwellers.

Some tenants could look back on long periods of regular attendance. As, for example:

	1633/4	*1637/8*	1641/2	*1654/5*
Richard Yates	18	12	16	18
Aaron Smith	14	16	17	18
John Dee	18	15	18	18
Richard Stringer	11	13	15	16
Henry Goble	..	16	15	18

Richard Yates was bailiff of the manor in 1630/1 and 1635/6 and probably in other years. We shall meet him serving on a committee inquiring into the water supply of Petworth, investing money as a mortgagee, acting as a guardian, and dealing in properties. He died holding by the courtesy of England a free tenement that had belonged to his wife Margaret. Aaron Smith served on the water committee and was a property owner in the town. His house in which he died in 1661 was Downams in North Street. John Dee was an ale-conner on several occasions. He lived in a tenement with a garden on which he borrowed £70 in 1650 and £50 in 1658. He repaid both loans on the due dates. Richard Stringer was a draper and mercer by trade and was prominent in manorial affairs serving as reeve and affeeror. He died in 1661. His son Richard was the founder of Stringer's Hall. Henry Goble was tenant of the Little White Hart. His father, who had been supervisor of the market conduit in the town water supply, owned a tenement in Back Street which became the arena for a violent quarrel over a right of way. All these matters are dealt with hereafter.

The seneschal of the manor, or the sub-seneschal, and sometimes both, presided or were present at the courts. They were appointed by the lord of the manor. But in administering the copyhold estate, in judging copyhold cases, and in entering the proceedings of the courts they had to be 'indifferent between the Lord and his tenants'. Below is a list of them during the seventeenth century so far as seems possible to complete it:

	Seneschal		*Sub-seneschal*
1595–1620	Sir Edward Francis[1]	1604–28	Richard Stokes
1620–43	Francis Poulton		
1644–48	Thomas Barnard		
1649–54	Hugh Potter	1649–53	Henry Champion
1654–73	Edward Thurland		
1673–83	John Dee		
1683–85	Henry Barnard		
1685–88	Henry Champion		
1689–93	Henry Barnard		
1694–1711	Thomas Beach	1694–1711	John Taylor

The bailiff of the manor also was appointed by the lord who usually farmed out the office. The same method was followed with 'the office of Bailiff or Portreeve and the Clerkship of the Market'. This carried with it:

> All and singular the butchers shambles, tolles and such profits, commodities, benefits, avayles and advantages whatsoever which Henry Wakeford late Bailiff had.

The lessee in January 1597 was William Levett at a rent

[1] Sir Edward was supervisor from 1605 while the 9th Earl was in the Tower.

of 53*s*. 4*d*. for twenty-one years. He was required, however, 'to repair the market house and other buildings and shambles'. When the time of expiry of his lease approached the 9th Earl wrote from the Tower an instruction that 'this should be let to the best advantage'. But the only relevant information on the subject is that the bailywick was farmed for £10 a year in 1617. Possibly the two offices were combined. They appear to have been so towards the end of the century when Jefferey Dawtrey is said to be both 'Bailiff of the Liberty' and 'Portreeve and Clerk of the Market'.[1]

The bailiff's duty was to execute the process of the court and we shall meet him distraining for fines and amercements and in two cases for felonies. He also collected the free and customary rents which in 1600 amounted to £64. 0*s*. 10*d*. made up as follows:

	£	*s*.	*d*.	£	*s*.	*d*.
Free tenants				14	12	8
Customary tenants:						
Petworth	14	6	3			
Northchapel	20	8	4			
Tillington	7	0	0			
Upperton	7	13	7			
				49	8	2
				£64	0	10

Another duty of his was to gather in the capons, gloves, cummin, and pepper which were part of some rents. In 1582 he prosecuted Richard Puttock for by his servants breaking into the pound and taking from it two geldings.

John Byrymble while serving as bailiff was accused in 1609 of having seven years previously misappropriated 'a piece of gold called an English sovereign worth 10[s]'. His accuser was John Goodwin who declared that he had

[1] Below, p. 31.

given Byrymble the sovereign to be added to the customary 'collection of benevolence of those who were present at the wedding' of John's son, who, so his father complained, had never received it. He had thus been deprived of a profit, which his father optimistically calculated to be 39*s.* 11¾*d.*

The reeve was the head of the homage or jury which usually numbered twenty-four who were sworn in by fours. The business of the court originated with them. They were required to present whatever happened in the manor to the prejudice of the lord or the tenants and to recommend what was of advantage to the lord without injury to the tenants. They stood thus intermediate between the lord and his tenants and bound to consider the interests of both. Hence a recommendation by them accepted by the court was considered to be binding on all tenants and on the lord.

The messor was responsible for the lord's court perquisites and amercements: as, for example, the fines and heriots recoverable on the estate transactions of copyholders, reliefs due on freeholds, and royalties on the mining of iron ore. He or the Hayward superintended the water meadows and commons. At times he was given tasks more fitting for the bailiff, as on the occasion when he was ordered to seize the Laces copyhold near Colehook Mill[1] which widow Magicke attempted to let without a licence contrary to custom. Three years afterwards her son surrendered it to the lord. A Hayward replaced the Messor for the nine years 1651–60, again in 1684, and thereafter. No reason is given for this change.

The ale-conners were kept busy reporting sales of beer on short measure and were responsible also for detecting breaches of the assize of bread and sales of butter on short weight. So also the searchers and sealers of leather were guardians of the public against adulterated forms of that

[1] Map VI.

commodity. The registrar recorded the genuine product. In 1658 John Gander counterfeited the seal and was amerced 40*s*. for the offence. This deplorable escapade is the only known fact concerning him. The Palesters of the Great and Little Parks were sinecurists, survivors of the old feudal service of paling so many perches of the lord's park.

Affeerors, whose duty it was to settle the amount of an amercement and if necessary to reduce it to an equitable sum, were appointed irregularly before the middle of the seventeenth century when their consistent appearance coincided with an appeal by the tenantry to the Chancery court. The only references to this in the Court Books are two presentments against Henry Sadler, of Cradlers or Cradlefield in Upperton, in 1644 and 1645 for 'keeping a decree made in Chancery between the Lord and his tenants from the Homage'. He was ordered to produce it before the next court. He did not obey and the command had to be repeated a year later reinforced by a penalty of £5 which he never paid.[1]

Henry Sadler was an unsatisfactory tenant in other ways and a victim of the mortgage rash. The year after he had succeeded to the house, garden, barn, and 24 acres of Cradlers he raised £60 on them from Leonard Rooke an active mortgagee. In 1642 he increased this to £80 by a transfer to William Savage. In 1646/7 he added £40 more with John Levett who took over the whole sum of £120, despite the fact that the year before the buildings had been reported to be ruinous. Sadler was ordered to repair them before the feast of St. John the Baptist under a penalty of 5*s*. He failed either to repair or to pay and so was presented again. Perhaps he did then carry out some superficial repairs, for complaints against him did not recur until 1655 when the premises were said to be in

[1] There is no record of this decree at Petworth or at the Public Record Office. For Sadler's Cradlers see map X and below, pp. 91–2.

decay. Nevertheless he was not amerced. On the other hand, John Levett decided to foreclose.

The primary function of the court in its customary capacity was the administration of the manorial copyhold estate. A copyholder was forbidden to let his tenement for more than a year and a day without licence of the lord issued by the court for a moderate fine; and a licence was not granted for more than seven years. For longer terms a renewal was necessary at the end of each seven-year period. All transfers of copyholds, whether by descent or alienation, whether absolute or conditional, came before the court and the same procedure was followed. The copyholder had to surrender the tenement into the hands of the lord in court, or, if physically unable to do so, he could surrender it to two or three of his fellows who were bound to present the fact at the next court. If they failed in this duty they committed a serious offence as did William and John Jackson of Tillington in 1693. The conditional surrender of widow Chalcroft had been made to them when she mortgaged her cottage, garden, and half-acre in Lurgashall parish to Thomas Warner the miller. They omitted to present the surrender at the next court and knowledge of it emerged only when Warner foreclosed after the widow's death. Forfeiture of their copyholds was the penalty for their carelessness. But it was not enforced; and a few years later they surrendered their tenements to the lord apparently without constraint.

The next step after a surrender was a proclamation repeated if necessary at two subsequent courts inviting claimants for admission. In reply the heir, or the widow, or the purchaser came and made his or her claim. If it was accepted admission followed subject to the payment of a fine due to the lord. Sometimes an estate lay dormant in the hands of the lord because of inability to pay the fine, or because no heir or other applicant appeared. Such a dispute had occurred at the court held on 1 October

1372, when Richard Wade and his wife Joan complained that Edward Sokedame had deprived them of two cottages formerly held by Joan's father, Stephen Bush. Edward argued that the cottages had been proclaimed at several courts after Stephen's death without anyone applying for admission, and that the lord of the manor had thereupon conceded one to him. He disclaimed any interest in the other and appealed to the court rolls to justify him. In reply Richard and Joan upheld that even if the cottages had remained in the lord's hands for some time that should not affect their plea seeing that Joan was 2½ years old when her father died in 1348, while the custom of the manor required that with an heir of tender age and 'in unknown parts' no failure to respond to a proclamation should debar his right. To this Edward retorted that Joan was resident within the lordship when her father died and yet neither she nor anyone on her behalf had claimed the premises until now after twenty-four years. To this shaft Joan and her husband had nothing to say. No decision was taken and the case was referred to at three subsequent courts only to be adjourned. It seems probable, therefore, that Edward remained in possession.

If a property were mortgaged, a very common circumstance in the seventeenth century, it was surrendered conditionally and the mortgagee was admitted on paying part of the fine due on an absolute surrender and with the condition that he restore the premises to the mortgagor when the loan was repaid. The mortgagor did not then need to be readmitted as he had never ceased to be the legal tenant. If the mortgagee foreclosed he had on admission to pay the balance of the full fine.

The seventeenth century witnessed a rash of mortgaging. During the ninety years between 1628 and 1717 the copyholders (there are no available figures for the freeholders) raised approximately £16,750 by this means.

The movement started before 1628, but only fitfully. The figures for each decade thereafter were:

	£
1628–37 . .	945
1638–47 . .	1,575
1648–57 . .	2,105
1658–67 . .	3,180
1668–77 . .	1,290
1678–87 . .	1,540
1688–97 . .	1,860
1698–1707 . .	1,860
1708–17 . .	2,395
	£16,750

All this business passed openly through the court and became public after being presented. Before that formality it was confidential and to publish it was a breach of privilege. Thus Peter Quennell, of a family interested in the leather trade,[1] was amerced 2*s.* 6*d.* in 1670 'for going out of our Jury and disclosing our secret and publishing it before it was brought a presentment into Court'. The manorial record, however, did not disclose the rent due on a lease nor the price paid for an absolute surrender. On the other hand, the sum advanced on a mortgage with the rate of interest and the date of repayment were always stated. Mortgaging was a business carried on locally between neighbours, and the wide diversity of those who were mortgagees is shown in the list of tradesmen who invested their savings in this class of security (see table opposite). In one instance only can the sum raised be related with moderate confidence to the improvement it financed. The £50 borrowed by the widow of Geoffrey Goodier in 1671 on the security of a tenement called Churchmans in West Street and 15 acres at Limbo.[2] She appears to have spent it on rebuilding the house, for thereafter it is referred to as 'lately rebuilt'.

[1] Peter Quennell was ten times a searcher and sealer between 1640 and 1677; John Quennell was registrar five times during the same period. His son John was a searcher and sealer nine times between 1673 and 1698.

[2] Map VIII.

Trade	*Numbers*	*Total advanced*
		£
Apothecary	1	145
Blacksmith	3	470
Bricklayer	1	30
Butcher	2	280
Carpenter	2	110
Cook	1	10
Draper	2	125
Gingerbread baker	1	20
Glover	1	20
Innkeeper	2	150
Mercer	1	500
Saddler	1	50
Shoemaker	1	32
Tallow chandler	1	250
Thatcher	1	40
Tailor	1	100
Tobacco-cutter	1	70
Wheelwright	2	250
	25	£2,652

Though a copyholder formally held his estate at the will of his lord, the common law had endowed him with a heritable title terminable only by escheat through lack of an heir or by reason of a felony. Moreover he held his tenement for an unalterable and derisible rent fixed in ages past when money had a higher value, and for a similarly anachronistic commutation of the labour services formerly due by his villein ancestors. If he died intestate, as was usual, his estate descended to his youngest son by the custom of borough-English. His widow, however, if espoused as a virgin, was entitled to a dower of at least a third of it as her 'free bench'. In the Petworth manor her bench, with few exceptions, was the whole.

Both customs of borough-English and widow's bench could be evaded. A widow's claim was limited to the tenements her husband possessed at death. She was deprived by a previous sale or by the estate having been entailed without including her life interest. When Thomas

Noel died in 1687, having surrendered his cottage at Colehook to himself for his life with remainder to his son Edward, without conferring a life interest on his wife Anne, she had no bench. By mistake she was admitted to it; but a marginal note in the Court Book points out the error. A widow had to defer also to the right of a mortgagee. On the other hand, a mortgagee would not necessarily stand on his right to exclude her. The estate of 54 acres in Upperton, of which William Marks was the copyholder in 1610,[1] had been reduced to a house and 2 acres and a plot in Budham Mead by mortgages when his descendant John Marks died in 1640. And these were pledged to Henry Kelly for £30. But he left the widow in peace for fifteen years.

The youngest son too could be dispossessed of his customary inheritance by an entail, or by his father surrendering the estate to the use of his will nominating another heir. Henry Goble in 1670 by will devised his new-built stables and his garden in White Hart Lane in Petworth[2] to his wife for her life and then to John his elder son on condition that he paid his younger brother William £100 at his coming of age. William Stempe on his death-bed in 1567 surrendered his cottage, measuring 25×18 ft. to his younger son John aged six for his life with remainder to his elder son Robert and his heirs. John therefore succeeded to a life interest only in the cottage. To the rest of the estate, consisting of three crofts, he was adjudged to be heir by custom. But he was kept out by his mother's bench. In 1571 Robert Belchamber, 'being near his death', divided his property near Northchapel, consisting of Garlands, 80 acres, and Shonks, 15 acres, between his sons John and Robert. The division was easy as the two were separated by Stephen Ede's Homdene. To the elder John he surrendered Shonks, leaving Garlands to descend to the younger Robert, thus

[1] Map X. [2] Below, p. 131.

adhering to custom in so far as he made the younger his principal heir.[1] Richard Stringer, the founder of Stringer's Hall in East Street, is another example. Dying childless he left his estate to his niece Susan Cook in preference to her two brothers of whom Richard the younger was the customary heir.[2] William Rogers, in September 1658, 'being sick and weak', surrendered his messuage and 4 acres at Limbo to his son William, but with the saving clause that the surrender should be void if he recovered. In these circumstances no fine was imposed nor was a heriot taken, as there was no animal. The first proclamation was made, but as it was not repeated he would seem to have recovered and resumed possession.

A widow having the whole property as her bench was not inconvenient as the custom of borough-English encouraged the succession of infants whose mothers were the natural guardians at any rate of their bodies. Otherwise a family relative to whom the property could not descend was preferred, or someone nominated by the deceased parent, or, for want of anyone having such a qualification, 'some honest man chosen by the homage'. A guardian was bound to answer for the fine payable on the infant's admission, for the ancient rent and labour commutation, for the repair of the house, for the convenient upbringing of the infant and, on his reaching his majority, for paying him any overplus of the profits received during the guardianship.

A heriot was due to the lord on all descents and alienations of copyholds, except on the death of a widow 'being a bencher for life'. If an estate consisted of two or more copyholds the lord could claim a heriot on each. But heriots, of course, depended upon an available animal. Often there was none. Sometimes nothing but an old mare, or 'a pig because there was no better animal', would be seized. The frequent return 'no live beast' is evidence

[1] Map III.

[2] Below, p. 132.

of many disappointments. In rare cases a cash equivalent had become customary. On a cottage the usual heriot was 2*d.* The heriots when Roger Heal was admitted to a rood of land near Tillington and when William Ford of Pippets was admitted in 1571 to his part of Inholmes[1] were proved *per antiqua copia* to be 6*d.* On John Ubbley's tenement near Lane's Garden in East Street[2] it was 16*d.* by custom. One collected on a garden and two crofts was assessed at 6*d.* because there was no cottage on them. Of course on many properties valuable heriots were seized.

A relief was due on the descent of a free tenancy and there were rare instances of one being paid on an alienation. The Rev. Thomas Mandeville, Rector and lord of Petworth Rectory Manor from 1531 until 1560, claimed the right to a relief and a heriot on both these occasions. But by an agreement made with thirteen of his tenants he abandoned the heriots and was content with a relief equal to one year's rent on descents while the tenants agreed to pay a relief also on alienations. Despite the failure of his Rector on the heriot issue the 7th Earl in 1558 attempted to seize two heriots on the death of Thomas Bowyer of London, one of his free tenants. Their collection was delayed on the heir stating that 'his deeds would defend the same'. But they were still outstanding in 1559. That same year John Turges died holding two copyholds and three freeholds. One of the freeholds was described as being 'in the market near the cross'. But the cross had disappeared before 1610, for a neighbouring tenement is then identified by the remark that 'sometimes a cross stood near it'. The Earl got his heriots on the copyholds but a note on the court roll records that the heriots on the freeholds had been stayed

[1] The fields marked V–XIII in map XIIB are occasionally labelled Inholmes or Inholmes closes. Which is here referred to is uncertain. In 1610 all were demesne except VI. For Pippets see below, pp. 137–8.

[2] For Lane's Garden see below, p. 131.

by advice of his counsel. On the other hand, a heriot of a cow worth 75*s*. was taken when John Smith inherited the freehold tenement called Tanners Land from his father Thomas in 1579.[1] But this appears to be an exception proving the rule. A century and a half later the Duke of Somerset tried to seize heriots on transfers of tenements in socage and got the opinion of Thomas Lutwyche, a distinguished lawyer, then Treasurer of the Inner Temple and a member of Parliament. He could do no more than declare the matter to be a question of custom depending on satisfying a jury. He gave, however, a definite opinion that heriots were not necessarily due on freeholds because they were leviable on copyholds.

The feudal aids due on making the lord's son a knight and on the marriage of his eldest daughter were not exacted in Sussex. Only a relief was payable on the succession of an heir of full age. According to a statement it was assessed on the scale ranging from 1⅞*d*. for 1 acre, or a 640th part of a full knight's fee of £5. Under this scale the hide was 160 acres and the virgate 40; but a note added that where the virgate was but 30 acres the relief for every acre was 2½*d*., the scale thus reaching the full £5 at 480 acres. By the sixteenth century reliefs had been established as equal to one year's fixed rent. The lord had a right to the custody and wardship of an infant heir of a freehold tenant, and to a fine on his marriage. John Smith in 1581 was subjected to both these feudal survivals,[2] and they were not abolished until the restoration in the next century.

The fines payable on descents and alienations of copyholds, being arbitrary and not governed by custom, depended upon what the lord was willing to accept and what the claimant for admission was able to pay. They had to be 'reasonably set and agreed upon' and the claimant had

[1] Below, pp. 94–5. John Smith inherited nine freehold tenements, seven of them within the precincts of the town.

[2] Below, p. 96.

a remedy in the courts. In rare cases they had become fixed. Thus Henry Barnes was able to produce copies of court rolls of 21 and 23 Henry VIII proving that the fine on a tenement and garden in East Street had been settled by custom at 16*d.* When Henry Hamlin in 1586 surrendered Megrams, 20½ acres in Tillington, to Joshua Masters, an infant aged ten, the fine was fixed by the special grace of the lord for this and any future succession or alienation at not more than 2*s.* 8*d.* The experience of the Hawkins family is an apposite example of the usual practice.

When Geoffrey Hawkins died in 1611 as copyholder of his village tenement and 36 acres in Upperton[1] his son Thomas lost a cow valued at 40*s.* which was seized as a heriot. He paid also a fine of £26. 13*s.* 4*d.* When Thomas died in 1642 the heriot was an ox worth £3. 15*s.* 0*d.* and the fine for his widow Anne entering on her bench was £22. Her youngest son Matthew surrendered the reversion to his elder brother John on condition that John paid him an annuity of £8 during Anne's life and £12 thereafter. John, however, did not live to inherit, and when Anne died in 1672 her eldest son George became the copyholder. He at once settled the estate on himself and his own son George. But both son and father died six months later in the plague of that year, leaving George's sister Mary, an infant aged two, as the heiress. She and Mary, her mother and guardian, were thus faced with an accumulation of death duty: three fines assessed at £30 each. Those due on the deaths of her father and her brother were halved in consideration of the circumstances while the fine for the guardianship was settled at £20, making £50 in all—a heavy drain. But no heriots were taken on the three transfers.

Another fine, this time on a reversion, concerned a tenement near North Street owned in her own right by

[1] Map X.

Jane Morris. Phillis Moody, her sister, was admitted to the reversion in March 1650 on a fine of 20*s.* and thereupon transferred it to Aaron Smith thus presenting the lord with a second fine of 20*s.* Four months later Jane and her husband John settled the property on themselves for life with remainder to Phillis Moody and then to Aaron Smith. In the margin of the Court Book is an explanation that no fine was charged on this last transaction as one had been levied on the surrender of Phillis Moody to Smith.

Difficulty in meeting fines sometimes caused long delays in admissions during which the copyhold remained in the hands of the lord. Richard Ede in 1617 took three months to raise the £40 needed to secure his admission to Redlands which he had bought from William Christmas.[1] The same interval elapsed before Gerson Butcher could get possession of a tenement in East Street, part of Lane's Garden. So also the transfer of Christopher Flower's cottage[2] and garden in Northchapel to Henry Pullen was refused as the fine was not forthcoming after the third proclamation. Other transferees abandoned the search. When John Flower of Beales, Steers, and Combers passed the 23 acres of Beales to his son John in 1615, John failed on the fine and John Rapley was the next occupant.[3]

Nicholas James in 1650 was rashly admitted to a messuage, garden, barn, and croft of 1½ acres in East Street before he had paid the fine of £15. Three months later he mortgaged the property to Anne Page for £120; she did not, apparently, realize the hollowness of her security. The fine was still unpaid in 1652 although 'reasonably set and agreed upon'. Moreover he added to his offence by obstinately refusing to render any account of the revenue

[1] Below, pp. 82–3.

[2] Map IV, no. 13.

[3] For Beales, Steers, and Combers see maps I, III, and below, pp. 77 and 79.

derived from the property. A seizure was therefore ordered. Thereupon Anne paid the fine and foreclosed. She had before paid £3 on the conditional mortgage surrender. Another seizure in similar circumstances was ordered to be enforced by the Reeve in 1651 after William Sadler had been admitted to Thomas Humphrey's estate in Upperton. In this case the threat was effective and he paid the fine. But in 1655 his barn was reported to be ruinous and two years later a second seizure was pronounced because he allowed part of his buildings to be removed without a licence.[1]

Remissions of fines were more frequent than distraints. John Payne had paid 20*s.* to secure a cottage and garden at Crosole.[2] When he died in 1689 his widow entered on her bench for 3*s.* 4*d.* 'in respect of her poverty'. Jane Howden as a widow was admitted in 1616 to a tenement and garden in North Street, despite her inability to pay the fine. Several other cases could be cited.

Towards the end of the sixteenth century the 9th Earl had serious disputes with his copyholders over the enclosures into the park made by his father and himself. They are dealt with in Chapter III. Together with this major grievance the tenants complained about the assessment of fines, and the seizure of heriots, while the Earl objected to the custom of guardianship as it was applied. The tenants carried the battle, during which they did much damage to fences and enclosures, to the Court of Chancery. In the course of the lengthy subsequent proceedings they made the offer that all fines on descents and alienations should be assessed on the basis of two years annual value of a tenement. The court considered this a 'very liberal offer' and the Earl accepted it, at the same time declaring that he would be content with less. Accordingly a Chancery decree declared that for evermore

[1] For the Humphrey copyhold in Upperton see map X.

[2] See map XIIB.

fines on descents and alienations should not exceed two years value, or one year for a widow entering on her bench. Nevertheless, despite the eternity given to the order, no attention appears to have been paid to it and fines continued to be assessed as before on what the lord would accept and what the applicant could pay.

On heriots the tenants argued that the lord could seize only cloven-hoofed beasts unless the dead copyholder had possessed only such as were round-hoofed. On this the evidence of the rolls was clearly against them and the lord was assured of the right to seize the best beast, be it cloven- or round-hoofed.

On the guardianship issue the Earl was judged to be wrong. He contended that an infant heir to a copyhold should not be admitted to his estate until he was of the full age of twenty-one for a male and eighteen for a female: and that during the minority the property should be the lord's to grant to whomsoever he chose without having to yield an account of the profits. This was a right he could exercise when the heir to a tenancy by knight service was a minor. An example of its potential value occurred in 1639 when the 10th Earl for £150 granted to Mary Avenol the custody, wardship, and marriage of John Avenol. He was the heir of his brother Thomas who had held Westland of 40 acres 'near Moore against Brinksole Heath' by the 40th part of a knight's fee, 1 lb. of pepper and erecting 4 perches of the Great Park pale. On his demise a mounter was delivered to the lord's stable. Mary was obliged:

1. To bring up and entertain John, 'his Lordship's ward', in good education, virtuous and decent qualities as to his Lordship's honour.
2. To save and defend all the inheritance of the ward and preserve the evidences, charters and writings of his estate.
3. Not to part with the wardship to any next of kin to whom the inheritance might descend.

4. Not to dispose of the ward in marriage where any cause of disparagement, detriment or annoyance might arise.
5. To abide by the order of the Earl concerning the money to be spent on the compositions, charges and disbursements of the wardship so that the ward should not be overcharged.

In support of his claim to apply this principle to copyholds the 9th Earl's counsel produced an exemplification of a verdict given in 1577. But as there was no record of this judgement nor any proof of it in the court rolls, and as rolls of Henry VIII, Philip and Mary, and of Elizabeth I supported the tenants the Chancery Court decreed:

1. That every infant within age should be admitted at the next court after the estate had fallen to him paying two years value as fine.
2. That his guardian should pay a small fine on being admitted as guardian.
3. That the guardian and his sureties should be bound in a competent sum to pay the fine and care for the infant's estate.

This implied maintaining the ward, paying the rent and doing no waste to the land, repairing the house when necessary, and accounting for the guardianship when the ward was of full age.

On these points the court specially mentioned the case of Bartholomew Farnedon. His father John had died in 1582 as the copyholder of 30 acres in Northchapel called Standish.[1] His mother died four years later as wife of Robert Butcher. Bartholomew was then aged fifteen. According to the entry on the court roll the tenement was then seized into the hands of the lord while the custody of Bartholomew's body was committed to his step-father until the next court. Arthur Shafto was then appointed guardian both of body and of land as 'an honest man

[1] This copyhold is not mentioned either in the terrier or in the map of 1610 under this name.

chosen by the homage'. Eleven years later the Chancery Court quoted him as having reduced Bartholomew to begging for want of maintenance while his house had been allowed to fall into great decay. It ordered an inquiry. What Arthur Shafto's position was in 1586, when he was appointed Bartholomew's guardian, is not known. After the finding of the court he is described as a yeoman and he became the tenant of the Lymes[1] for twenty-one years, but died four years later.

Another case in point concerned the guardianship of Richard Boxall of Wisdoms.[2] His father had died in 1628 since when his mother had been the bencher until her death in 1642. He was then aged seventeen. His brother-in-law Henry Collens, whose wife Elizabeth was Richard's heir, was his guardian. Was it proper then that the husband of the next heir should be the guardian of the infant to whom she might succeed? The court decided to retain him as guardian of the estate but on a fixed allowance of £5 a year. Moreover, 'if it shall appear that Henry Collens shall make any stripp (waste) upon the ground his guardianship to be void'. Richard's education was then entrusted to Anthony Sowter. These arrangements came to nothing as the ward died three months after his mother.

William Morris, who lived in East Street, was another guardian who failed in his trust. He had been specially nominated by the mother of the infant Richard Ford as she was dying in March 1612. She had been admitted to her bench in the tenement called Pippets in the street now known as High Street. It is specially marked in the 1610 map as the residence of William Ford. William was son of William, farmer of the demesne land for thirty-three years from 1547 to 1580. His grandson was now the infant

[1] The Lymes was a demesne farm of 29 acres near Petworth on the Kirdford road. Below, p. 50, and map VIII.

[2] For Wisdoms see map VI and below, p. 74.

heir.[1] The mother had been admitted to her bench only six months previously. Richard was admitted three weeks after her death had been presented and Morris was appointed the guardian on a substantial fine of £8. Eight years later the court was obliged to order the Messor to seize the property into the hands of the lord so that the bailiff should ensure a proper settlement of the estate.

At times the court bound a guardian to do certain things such as repairing buildings under the threat of a penalty. The ward's education also was sometimes specially mentioned. Thus Robert Strater was enjoined to educate at a suitable school William Morley the infant heir of Tillies, Brockhurst, and Bullreadings.[2] His father had hanged himself. Consequently the estate had been seized into the hands of the lord for a felony. It had then been reconceded to the younger son Robert who, dying soon afterwards, made way for his elder brother William's education.

[1] That Richard was the grandson of the first William is only a reasonable assumption. For Pippets see map XIIB.

[2] Map I.

2

THE MANOR

(2)

ALL the commons of the manor were north of Petworth town beginning with Petworth Common, now Hampers, measuring in 1610 8 acres. Next along the London Way came Hoads Common, as it still does, except that it was then Hoades and divided into two by a road now disused. Middlecarr, now Colehook, Common had been until the last decade of the sixteenth century an unenclosed wood. Its conversion into a common pasture played an important part in the dispute between the 9th Earl and his tenants over the enclosing of the park. It was in 1610 the largest common, covering 173 acres. Across the London Way on the site of the present Last Lodges was Copthurst Common of 13 acres. Adjoining the end of the northern arm of Middlecarr was Colehook Mill Common, of only 3½ acres. Chapel Common of 5 acres stretched eastward from Northchapel as it does still, though now less prominently. A similar highway common was Broad Street of 15 acres along the road to Shillinglee. In the opposite direction towards the west was Gospel Green of 5 acres, and from there to the south were Hillgrove 10 acres, Stony Lane near Parkhurst 6 acres, and Upperton Common 75 acres. In all 340 acres, or 5½ per cent. of the manorial total.[1]

Rights of common were either appendant or appurtenant. Common appendant was divided into parcels attached to particular tenements and confined to 'horses,

[1] For the commons see maps I, III, V, VI, VII, VIII, IX, and XV.

kine, beasts and sheep that were most fit for the plough'. Geese, goats, and hogs were not commonable on them. The valuable water meadows extending from west to east along the north bank of the Rother—Upper Mead, Budham Mead, Bridge Mead, Hole Mead, Mill Mead, Wide Mead, and Holebroke Mead[1]—were of this class. The several portions in them were annually demarcated by the tenants. In 1641 those of Upper Mead were ordered in July to perform this duty within six days under a penalty of 5*s*. In September they were commanded to repair the fences and clean out the ditches, the penalty being doubled. A year later they had to be chivied again and the fine was increased to 40*s*. In 1644 it was 50*s*. On the other hand the tenants of Budham Mead responded to the first order.

William Sturt, who was Messor 1600–2, neglected his duties as supervisor of the commons and meadows, and in October 1601 he was amerced 2*s*. 3*d*. for this. In the following March he was penalized 3*s*. 4*d*. for not superintending Wide and Budham Meads and allowing pigs and transport animals to pasture on them. In June he committed the still more serious offence:

> That he did the night before he went to drive the commons send word to them that were the encroachers to keep out their cattle out of the common.

This cost him 2*s*. 6*d*. more. Finally, in October he was fined another shilling for allowing horses and other transport animals on Wide Mead. In all therefore he paid 9*s*. 1*d*. for his delinquencies, not an unreasonable punishment.

Other commons were appurtenant to the commoners in general as was declared by the homage early in the eighteenth century:

> We present that the herbage is the tenants' by the mouth of

[1] Maps XIII and XIV.

the cattle and all fern and heath and bushes that grow upon the waste they ought to have it without licence of the Lord to spend it upon the premises and not elsewhere.

No one shall turn out any beast or cattle having no liberty upon the common, if such do to pay 2*s.* 6*d.*

A copyholder could not let his common right as did Robert Fulwyke in 1561, an offence for which he was presented but not amerced. All manner of beasts 'rising and lying' on a tenant's lands were commonable except goats and geese. In 1630 Mary Finch, widow of Anthony Finch,[1] and John Goodier, who was of *generosus* status and copyholder of Berdes,[2] were condemned for allowing their geese to graze on a common. Transport animals not used in farming operations were barred. Hogs were allowed only when ringed and yoked. In 1669 Philip Willard of Upperton and John Sadler of North Readings[3] put hogs unringed and unyoked on Upperton Common and were each condemned to a fine of 10*s.* if the hogs were not ringed and yoked before the next court.

The carrying capacity of a common was a matter of general knowledge or custom and the court had no difficulty in amercing copyholders who overgrazed. Anyone could be called upon to prove his right, as was William Holmes, who was not a tenant of the manor, when his cattle were found on Hoads Common in 1703. In 1632 five copyholders were presented for grazing where they had no right: and John Huckman of Lurgashall was fined 10*s.* for trespassing with his sheep and his mare on Upperton Common. Petty encroachments by copyholders were vigilantly pilloried by the court, not always successfully: as with Richard Galer. In 1642 he was amerced 10*s.* for encroaching on the lord's waste. He took no notice. A year later the amercement was renewed. Again he did nothing. Finally, in 1645, after three years of

[1] For Anthony Finch see below, p. 88.

[2] Map III.

[3] Map IX.

illegal occupation, he was fined 5*s.* and allowed to remain in possession for his life at a rent of 4*d.*

The lord was willing enough with the consent of the homage to license the building of a cottage on his waste. He was the more encouraged if the request were supported by a reasonable number of tenants declaring as they did on behalf of William Jackson in 1582 that conceding him half a rood at the Leith[1] for this purpose would not be detrimental. Jackson therefore was admitted, but only as a life tenant paying a rent and a fine of 6*d.* Four years later Thomas Mason in similar circumstances was granted a plot 4 perches square near Ragham[2] as a copyhold at a rent of 8*d.* and a fine of 3*s.* 4*d.* In 1614 he was given a second copy of court roll, having lost the old one. Nicholas Good in 1630 and John Boxall in 1648 were treated in the same way. Good was backed by his fellow parishioners of Lurgashall and was licensed to enclose 4 perches, formerly occupied by William Thorncomb but now in the lord's hands, and to build a cottage on them as a life tenant. The fine for this was 10*s.* and the rent 12*d.* John Boxall was admitted, also on the humble petition of Lurgashall, to a cottage which the lord had licensed Thomas Booker to build and which was now vacant. His fine was 20*s.* and his rent 12*d.* The case of Giles Morgan was similar. He had, presumably on a licence, enclosed and made a garden of a bit of waste at Gunters Bridge, had built a cottage on it, and was now granted possession for a fine of 6*s.* 8*d.* On his death it passed to his widow as her bench and finally to his daughter Alice on a fine of 10*s.* Northchapel, too, in 1657 got up a petition in support of John Burle's prayer to be admitted formally to a cottage he had lately built on the waste at Colehook, and he became the copyholder at a rent of 12*d.* without

[1] The Leith was on the right of the Byworth road going from Petworth. The Little Leith was on the left. Map XVI.

[2] Map XV.

a fine. But soon afterwards he had to be condemned to a penalty of 10*s.* if a second encroachment he had ungratefully committed were not undone before the next court. John Sherlock also became the copyholder in 1638, for a fine of 5*s.* and a rent of 12*d.*, of a garden which he had enclosed and a cottage he had built on the waste at Colehook. On his death a year later his son succeeded and so brought a second 5*s.* to the lord. A third 5*s.* accrued when he died within a year and his infant son aged ten was admitted.

John Upfold neglected to get a licence for a cottage he had built on a parcel of waste at Chilnhurst in 1630. This omission and his failure to pull down the cottage was presented to the court general. He was not amerced and was allowed to stay, but he got no title. The experience of John Payne, the poverty of whose widow was mentioned in the last chapter, furnishes also an example of the arbitrariness of fine. In 1654 he erected a smithy on the lord's waste at Crosole without a licence and was amerced 6*d.* for the offence. In 1655 he was charged 4*d.* more for building a cottage next to the smithy. In 1656 another penny was added to these amercements making 11*d.* in all. Then in December of that year his ownership was established at a yearly rent of 6*d.* and a fine of 6*d.* Hence in 1661 he was able to surrender the smithy and the cottage to Michael Boad, for what sum is not mentioned, but the fine on the transaction was assessed at 10*s.* Nine years later he bought back the cottage, but for his readmittance he had to pay 20*s.* And there he lived until he died, leaving an impoverished widow. The site is now occupied by a barn and cottage attached to Frog Farm.

The timber on a copyhold and the minerals under it were the lord's. To fell a tree without his licence was a serious offence. It might involve a forfeiture of the land on which it had been committed with restoration on a fine of six times the value of the timber.[1] The lord, however, was bound to assign to a tenant the customary housebote or timber for building or repairs, and ploughbote to repair his wagons, carts, ploughs, and instruments of husbandry. A tenant had a right also to firebote and hedgebote from the underwood on his land for his own fuel and hedges, but not for sale; and to the windfall of trees on his land, but he was not allowed to top or lop them. His right to windfall on commons was confirmed by the Chancery court. A roll of 33 Henry VIII demonstrated that for a copyholder to take such windfall without licence was prejudicial to the lord and to the tenants. Another of 4 Edward VI amerced one of the Bowyers for appropriating the windfall of three trees contrary to the custom of the manor which limited the right to one tree only. The court was satisfied from this roll that there was a custom concerning windfalls in the commons, while the other roll proved that taking windfall could be prejudicial to the tenants as well as to the lord. This it could not be if the tenants had no interest in windfalls. Furthermore, fifteen witnesses had testified that time out of mind one load had been the custom. The court therefore decreed that the tenant who first found a windfall on a common and marked it, unless it were on that part of a common which was within the park called Petworth Park, should have the right to one load of one tree. Incidentally this appears to be the first official use of the term 'Petworth Park'.

Sitting as a Leet the manorial court was primarily concerned with its unending struggle to cleanse the streets of the town. A pillory[2] had stood in the Market Place though no report survives of anyone having been placed in it. In 1559, when Margaret Redcroft died, she occupied a shop

[1] See the case of Mary Stent below, p. 76.

[2] Among the liberties claimed by Eleanore Plantagenet in 1272 as widow of Henry 9th Baron de Percy and as Lady of the Manor of Petworth were the assize of bread and of beer, and of pillory and tumbril (cucking stool). (Percy Chartulary, 378/9.)

'near the pillory', and when her son died in 1571 the pillory was still in position. So it was, apparently, when Arthur Levett had a shop 'against the pillory' in 1621. It is not mentioned again. In 1674, four centuries after Eleanore Plantagenet, the Court pressed for the purchase of a cucking stool, and eight years later for a whipping post; two requests frequently repeated without result.

In 1612 two copyholders were amerced 8*d*. each for forestalling butter and eggs coming to the market. But these were the only prosecutions for this offence. The main complaint was summed up in a general presentment offered in September 1644:

> That the streets and highways of the town are foul and full of dung and dirt to the common nuisance of the King's people in default of the inhabitants of the said town and therefore [we] do order that every inhabitant within the said town shall amend and reform the said nuisance so much as concerns every inhabitant respectively upon pain of every particular person as shall be found defective to forfeit 20*s*. to be amended before the feast day of All Saints next.

Again in 1689:

> We present all who throw their dirt into the street without laying it in a heap in a convenient place and do amerce them 6*d*. each.
>
> We present the foulness of all the Market Place and all along the church style[1] and we give the dung to Jeffery Dawtrey Bailiff of the liberty and do amerce him 10*s*. if it be not cleaned and carried away every month.

The complaint had to be repeated in 1690. Moreover, Jefferey Dawtrey had been arraigned in 1678 because

> as Portreeve or Clerk of the Market he does not keep the market house clean, and that if the dung and every 'noysum' thing be not carried away by next court and the market house 'steares'

[1] The church stile was the present south entrance to the churchyard.

be not boarded up close at his charge to prevent the 'noysumnes' of it, he to be amerced 10s and for the future to keep it very clean and the market place swept clean once a week upon a penalty of 5s for any neglect.

In 1691 the Court passed a condemnation of 'all dunghills, logs and rubbish lying about the town to offend neighbours' adding a general amercement of 2*s*. 6*d*. In 1692 the southern end of North Street was particularly condemned as being 'noisome to the people'. Adam Austin was held responsible and was amerced 2*s*. 6*d*. if he did not clean it up before the next court. At the same time the Rector, the Rev. Edward Pelling, D.D., was reported for having two great logs lying against the east gate of the churchyard.

The wandering hogs and the numerous pigsties in the town were not conducive to cleanliness and were impossible to eradicate. In 1642 the townspeople were warned to keep their swine off the streets and Market Place under a penalty of 6*d*. for each pig. Previously the fine had been calculated in the gross, as it was when Richard Aylwyne, the brewer, had been amerced 2*s*. 6*d*. for an unspecified number of vagrants. In 1655 the 6*d*. was reinforced by 4*d*. for feeding pigs in the streets. Thereafter other changes followed. In 1658 the 4*d*. was applied to pigs unringed and unyoked and without a herder. The next year thirteen, including Henry Sadler the butcher, earned this penalty. Then in 1662 the following ordinance was promulgated:

> Ordered that Robert Tredgrove and Francis Hayward be appointed by this Court, with the consent of the homage and the tenants present, to drive all the pigs that wander about the street to the pound and that they shall have 4d for each hog they do so impound to be paid by the owner of the hogs.

The first year afterwards showed an improvement, with only four culprits. But the following three years each produced fourteen or fifteen and no pig was impounded. Hence a new order that:

> All who keep hogs unringed and unyoked and suffer them to come into the street shall for every such offence forfeit 6d.

In 1671 this fine was raised to 8*d.* per pig per day and impounding was again insisted on. A repetition of this order in 1677 was no more effective. Nor was raising the fine to 12*d.* in 1685. The pig problem still survived in the nineteenth century.

Pigs naturally implied pigsties and the court was vigilant against 'erecting hog pens near the highway to the annoyance of the passengers', or 'a hog stye near the king's highway in the town'. Robert Trewe, the maltster, was amerced 4*d.* for this in 1661. Henry Sadler, the butcher, even established a *caula porcilica ad murum ecclesiae*. For this he was adjudged to pay 5*s.*

The same trouble arose over the placing of 'houses of office' or privies near the street, and the court had to order their removal to some more remote site.

The many presentments for dunghills and rubbish heaps, for stone, mortar, timber, logs, and faggots in the streets or highway, for overflowing water from cisterns or other sources, particularly of dye water from the two dyehouses, for travelling wagons left standing all night, and for the romantic misdemeanour of 'casting sheep's horns into the street' show how solicitous, and how ineffective, the court was as a sanitary authority. It had to depend on the householders from whom it was largely recruited and who themselves often committed the breaches it condemned.

A householder was responsible for repairing the pitching or pavement in front of his house as far as the gutter. In September 1680 the court ordered this work to be done by all within six weeks. Four years later the order was repeated and again in 1685. This time under the threat of 5*s*. for failure to comply. After repeating the command for two years more the court appears to have abandoned the struggle.

Amercements on tenants for selling beer 'with unlawful measures', not alone in Petworth but elsewhere in the manor, and among them some women, were a source of revenue until 1670. In that year they abruptly ceased. The court seems again to have tired of constantly repeating a penalty which was no deterrent and was less and less remunerative. During the last forty years of the long campaign against fraud an average of twenty-one tenants was annually presented for the offence. At Michaelmas 1630 seventeen were penalized as follows:

1 at 5*s*. 0*d*.	5*s*. 0*d*.
2 at 2*s*. 0*d*.	4*s*. 0*d*.
5 at 1*s*. 6*d*.	7*s*. 6*d*.
9 at 1*s*. 0*d*.	9*s*. 0*d*.
	£1. 5*s*. 6*d*.

Amongst those fined 1*s*. was Robert Trashe, who eight years before had inherited the musical instruments of his cousin Henry, the 'mussition'. These were tenor and treble violins valued at 42*s*.[1] Robert lived in a freehold tenement, sharing it with others. Later it became the cause of a war between two adjoining copyholds.

Faced with this malignant recidivism the court ordered that in future the fine should be 10*s*. But no attention was paid to this empty threat and the next year of sixteen offenders two paid 3*s*. each, three paid 2*s*., and eleven 1*s*. The ten-shilling penalty was never enforced. The highest was 2*s*. 6*d*., and that rarely, while most offenders got off with 1*s*. or 6*d*. Two ale-conners were elected annually to safeguard the public in this matter. Those serving in 1655 were ordered to report on it to the steward four

[1] I owe this information to Mr. G. H. Kenyon, who gathered it from the Chichester Inventories. See Chap. 6 for the war.

times a year under a penalty of 5*s.* But again this was bluff. When Richard Barnard and Henry Goble, despite his past regular attendance at courts, were found guilty in 1658 of disobeying this instruction they were fined 12*d.* and the next year Emery Puttock the elder[1] was let off for 6*d.* for the same omission. He had twice before acted as ale-conner. Thereafter the illicit trade continued to prosper and presentments for it reached twenty-six in 1664, while the revenue derived from them was derisory compared with that recovered from the seventeen delinquents in 1630:

4 at 1*s.* 0*d.*	. . . .	4*s.* 0*d.*
1 at 8*d.*	. . . .	8*d.*
1 at 6*d.*	. . . .	6*d.*
4 at 1*s.* 4*d.*	. . . .	5*s.* 4*d.*
16 at 2*d.*	. . . .	2*s.* 8*d.*
		13*s.* 2*d.*

The ale-conners were responsible also for the assize of bread. Complaints on this score were rare. A constant repetition of *omnia bene* dismisses it on the rolls. Nevertheless in 1630 William Rixon the Petworth baker was found guilty and condemned in 12*d.* 'for not making his bread of sufficient weight according to the Statute'. Moreover in 1670 the two ale-conners, Thomas Lucas, who more often served as a searcher and sealer of leather, and James Launder, were each fined 2*s.* 6*d.* for 'not weighing the bread and butter in the market as they ought to do'. Four years later John Mills, a baker from Midhurst, was caught selling under-weight in Petworth and was condemned to pay 3*s.* 4*d.* His offence drew another warning to ale-conners that they must weigh all bread exposed for sale.

The court was spasmodically alive to the risk of strangers securing settlements within the manor. To this end an order was promulgated in 1571 that no tenant

[1] Emery Puttock the younger served as a searcher and sealer of leather.

should receive anyone in his house who might become a charge on the neighbourhood. In 1587 three copyholders of Northchapel were convicted of disobeying this order and were each penalized 40*s*. if the intruders were not removed before Christmas. But no other cases occurred until the years 1616–18. Nicholas Martwick was then condemned to pay 10*s*. if the stranger he was harbouring in his cottage the London Way[1] end of the Five Rails Fence did not leave before the next court. Three other similar penalties had to be imposed. These inspired the court to issue two orders. The first decreed that only persons who lived honestly of their own without burdening their neighbours should be entertained unless the host found security protecting the town against liability under a penalty of 40*s*. Thereafter the court had no more concern with the Poor Law. Similarly presentments of copyholders who sublet parts of their tenements as a means of introducing strangers, a breach of custom if not licensed, did not recur.

One special function of the court was the upkeep of the water supply installed in Henry VII's reign. The town owed it to the Rev. John Edmonds, Rector for thirty-five years from 1496 to 1531. Leland has left a contemporary description of it:

> Parson Edmonds of late dayes, perceiving the great lak of water at Petteworth, causid chiefly a great spring, the hedde whereof is about a mile from the town, to be brought in lede to Petteworth: part of the water comming to the Manor Place and the residew to II or III places in the streate of the towne.

The spring is now enclosed within the paddocks of the park, but of old time it was on the north side of Hungers Lane as this passed by on its way to Snowhill and Upperton.[2] From the water house at the spring a leaden pipe connected with the main tap near the church stile and

[1] Map XV.

[2] See the Conduit Head in map XV.

from there two pipes supplied two market conduits, one in Market Place 'against ye common Inn ye George', the other at the north end of Sowter Street. In 1575 the water house and the pipes were reported to be 'in great decay'. This was not surprising after serving for at least seventy years. Thereupon the 8th Earl had agreed to share equally with the town the cost of repair. Supervisors of the church and of the market conduits were appointed and the town was endowed with the freehold of 7 acres called the Conduit Field[1] to provide an income to cover the cost of repairs. In 1625 the returns from the field were said to have sufficed for this purpose. Nevertheless great decay was again becoming manifest and a new agreement was necessary this time with the 9th Earl. By it he undertook to repair the water house and the pipes on three conditions: that the old pipes were to be his; that the Conduit Field should be added to his demesne; and that he should be allowed to install a fourth tap for the use of Petworth House. The 8th Earl had 'brought the water into every office of his house', but in the riots against the park enclosures the supply had been cut off. Apparently it had not been restored. There were other sources of supply.

The agreement imposed on the townspeople the duty of keeping their three taps in order and of assessing themselves for the cost. They reserved also the right to resume possession of the whole installation if the Earl defaulted. The supervisors were abolished and in their stead two wardens were appointed, one by the Earl and the other by the town. The acquisition by the town of a shop and a little new-built house near the church stile, which had belonged to the Smith family,[2] appears to have been connected with these appointments. The new wardens took charge and had power to give the Earl sixteen days' notice of what repairs were needed and these he had to

[1] Map XIIB, no. 26.

[2] Below, p. 94.

do within six months. The town and not the Earl failed. In September 1635 the homage ordered the conduit taps to be repaired at once and that a well called the Town Well should be maintained by an assessment on all who used it. A town well was not established. But for the repairs a committee, consisting of Daniel Morris the town conduits warden, Thomas Payne a free tenant, Richard Yates the bailiff, Richard Stringer the reeve, Aaron Smith, John Hall of New Grove, and Edward Peachey the haberdasher, whose son William married Mary Hall and so became possessed of New Grove,[1] was appointed with power to distrain for the sums assessed. Nevertheless, when the repairs had been completed there was no money to pay the workmen.

A year later the following minatory resolution was passed:

> Ordered with the consent of the Homage and the greater part of the inhabitants that the distress already taken of such persons as refused to pay the assessment and the distress hereafter to be taken shall be sold for the satisfaction of the assessment and the surplusage remaining after the sales to be delivered to them.

The next year a list of ninety-four persons who forfeited their several pains had to be published. Moreover, the breakdown in the rating system led to a misappropriation of charitable funds. The Rev. Nicholas Smith, Rector 1560–91, had given £20 as a fund to be lent to poor distressed tradesmen of the town and William Bradfold had added £10. It now appeared that Richard Stringer and Edward Peachey with Thomas Barnard, who afterwards served as sub-seneschal, and Edward Long, who lived in a house and garden called Davies in East Street and had been an ale-conner, the trustees of this fund, had spent it and £20 from the Parish chest on the water supply. A formidable array of eighteen of their fellow

[1] Below, pp. 124–5.

parishioners swore to these allegations and secured the appointment by the court of Chancery of a Commission of Enquiry under the Act for the Redress of the Mismanagement of Charitable Funds. The Commission, composed of five prominent local gentry, found the allegations proved, and that the £50 had been refunded. They further ruled that the £30 must be used as the donors intended and the £20 applied to some charitable purpose. For the water supply they confirmed the agreement of 1625 and declared that the money needed to repair the conduits should be assessed on the owners of houses and on others living in the town, including copyholders and lessees, 'according to their visible estates within the town'. Their report afterwards received the sanction of a Chancery decree dated 16 February 1641.

The cleanliness of the water taps was a frequent concern of the manorial court. It amerced, for example, Alery Coates 2*d*. for washing bullocks' entrails at one of the taps and warned her that a repetition of the offence would involve a penalty of 3*s*. 6*d*. A hundred years before watering horses and washing fish had been forbidden under a penalty of 3*s*. 4*d*., a high amercement compared with 2*d*. for entrails. The same remark might apply to a fine of 12*d*. imposed for washing roots. It was a serious offence to make an unofficial connexion with any of the pipes. Alice Martin,[1] when caught out in this, was fined 12*d*. and was ordered to remove her leaden pipe before the next court or pay 10*s*. The simplicity of Alice's will throws some light on her character. It was a direct document instructing her executors to sell all 'to persons willing to pay the best price'.

Such was the public water supply of the town, apart from the many private wells, for nearly three centuries until 1782. George, 3rd Earl of Egremont, then installed a pump at Coultershaw Mill, a reservoir, and supply pipes.

[1] For further information on Alice Martin see p. 125.

No connexion could be made to them without his consent, and users were responsible for keeping their branch pipes and their cocks in order. In 1839 they supplied 7 public cocks and 137 private taps, exclusive of those in Petworth House, owned by 69 persons.

The 'Gate of the Manor' in North Street was the entrance to the Mansion House of the lord. It is now the back

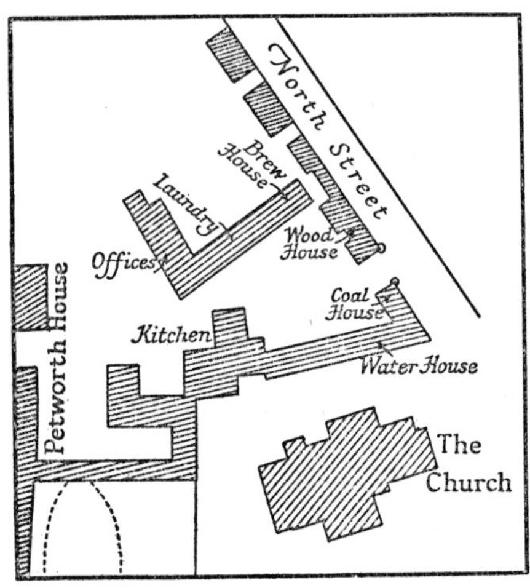

entrance to Petworth House. In 1537, when Henry VIII became lord of the Honour, 'a small chamber above the outer gate of the Manor' was reserved for the King's use as a 'larderhouse'.[1] The great stone posts and the outhouses surrounding the court to which they give access were built by the 9th Earl. The ground plan is reproduced above. The plan in principle remains the same today, but two of the buildings are new. The brewhouse remained unchanged, though finally no longer brewing beer, until the end of the nineteenth century. It was then rebuilt and enlarged as a power-house. The wood house is now a lodge. The water house was connected with the town supply. It is now mainly used for coal and coke.

[1] P.R.O. Ministerial Accounts 3478. The plan is early eighteenth century.

The picture of the mansion is from the 1610 map, showing it as it was after the enlargements made by the 8th Earl. The most ancient relics of it today are the large vaulted beer cellar, dating at the latest from the fourteenth century, and the chapel facing east with its Early English arcades. The centre of the house was a great chamber or hall with an adjoining withdrawing chamber on the ground floor. These and the rooms occupied by Lord Percy[1] were near the chapel, the roof of which appears in the illustration beyond the central tower. Upstairs were the parlour, a room used for private conversation, and another withdrawing room. There were many other apartments, but the above are all that are needed for an account of the quarrel on 14 August 1620 between the 9th Earl's two sons-in-law: James Hay, Lord Doncaster, afterwards 1st Earl of Carlisle, and Robert Sydney, Lord Lisle, afterwards 2nd Earl of Leicester. It gives some insight into living conditions in the house.

Lisle arrived at Petworth on 13 August. The party there consisted of the 9th Earl, his son Lord Percy, Lord Doncaster, William Herbert, 3rd Earl of Pembroke, and his brother Philip, Earl of Montgomery. The next morning Lisle and Doncaster met in the upstairs withdrawing room where Doncaster's servants were pulling on his breeches and stockings. Their conversation, in which Lisle accused Doncaster of lack of courtesy towards him, ended in Doncaster calling Lisle a liar and Lisle responding with a blow. The conflict was then broken off by Lisle retiring from the field. Outside the door he met Peter Dodsworth, Lord Percy's man, whom he afterwards cited as a witness that he 'made no haste down the stairs'. He then went to Lord Percy in the cloister rooms and told him what had happened. His next visit was to the Earl, whom he found in bed. To him he expressed a desire to leave Petworth at once. But the Earl forbade

[1] Algernon, 10th Earl of Northumberland.

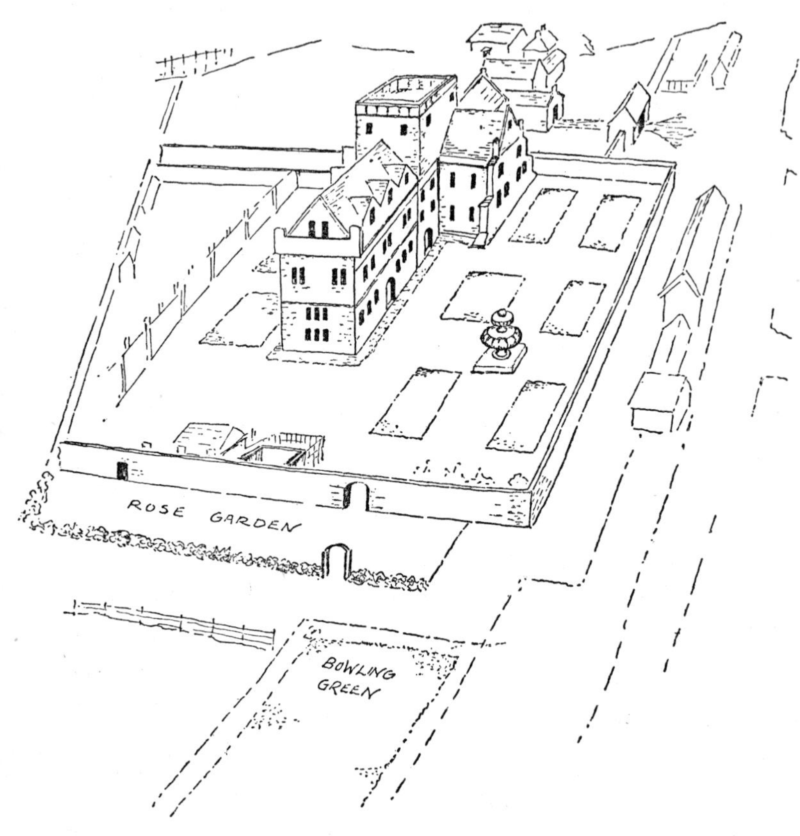

PETWORTH HOUSE 1610

From a drawing by R. G. Pidgley

him to do so and got up to try and negotiate a peace. Lisle then went back to Percy in the cloister where the Earl joined them after seeing Doncaster. All three then went out into the garden and saw Doncaster walking towards the bowling green. Lisle was thereupon ordered back into the house so as to keep the two combatants apart. He was naturally concerned that Doncaster should thus have opportunities to propagate his version of the affair, while he, Lisle, was denied similar freedom. He therefore dispatched James, Lord Percy's barber, to ask Percy to submit this consideration to the Earl. In reply he was told that he might go to the Birchen Walks with Percy. There the Earl came to them again but no record tells us what then transpired. At any rate they were now free to move towards the bowling green. But before they reached the rose garden they saw Doncaster and the others coming towards the house. So they turned thither, and as they entered it Sir Edward Francis whispered to Percy that the Earl desired Lisle to take off his sword as Doncaster was unarmed and might regard it as an affront. The company, now gathered in the Great Chamber, awaited the arrival of the Duke and Duchess [*sic*] of Buckingham[1] and other guests. Afterwards dinner passed without incident, the two combatants sat 'almost right against' each other, but 'neither took any notice of the other'. After dinner all returned again to the bowling green. But there was no bowling. Lisle and the less distinguished guests, who stood 'near the place where the bowls were kept', 'talked of nothing but bowling and the making of matches', while the others laboured with some success to patch up the quarrel.[2]

Beyond the bowling green was an orchard and between

[1] George Villiers was only Marquess of Buckingham in 1620. He was promoted to be Duke in 1623.

[2] This account of the quarrel is from the Sydney Papers, vol. I, pp. 121–7.

these two and West Street and the Court Ditch stretched the kitchen garden. Still farther to the west was the site on which the 9th Earl built the stables said by Defoe to be 'the finest in all the south of England and equal to some noblemen's whole houses'.

3

THE LORD'S DEMESNE

THE manor was a narrow irregular strip between the river Rother to the south and the Surrey border to the north. The land in it was divided between the lord's parks, his demesne and waste, the free tenants by knight service or socage, the customary tenants or copyholders, and the commons. The free tenants were comparatively unimportant as landowners. More than half their tenements were in the town absorbing little acreage. They were surveyed by William Stockdale in 1609. The proportions between the others in 1610, when Ralph Treswell made his great map of the manor, were:

	Acres
Parks	1,207
Demesne	3,794
Copyholds	3,010
Commons	340
	8,351

The parks and the commons were north of the town and there also were the woodlands and much virgin bush rated as inferior pasture awaiting development. To the south of the town and near Tillington and Upperton the land was free of such relics of the past, and outside the demesne was subdivided into strips suggesting an origin in the two-field system with scattered occupation.[1] The demesne immediately to the south of the town was set out in larger and more regular fields, and from 1460 to 1490 had been farmed out to William Ford of Pippets.

[1] Maps X and XIIB.

He was followed by three farmers. After 1507 there were four, of whom his son William was one, until 1519 when the number was reduced to three. A survey of 1557 shows that it was then occupied in severalty by eight tenants and that it was divided into thirty-two fields forming a block of 330 acres. Of these 252 were convertible—'sometimes sown and sometimes pasture'. They were 'good for both according to the soil and nature of the ground of that country'. Of the balance, 77 acres were good pasture and 1 acre, the Butt Croft, 'where a pair of butts standeth', was let as pasture. Afterwards, enlarged to 4½ acres, it became the football field. The mansion house with its hall, chambers, chapel, nursery, gatehouse, barns, stables, dovehouse, garden, and 'divers houses of office' occupied six acres. The thirty-two fields were distributed between the eight farmers:[1]

	Fields	*Acres*	*Character*
Thomas Sacher .	6	89	convertible
Richard Etherton .	8	66	,,
John Browne . .	6	51	,,
John Bease . .	2	42	,,
John Young . .	4	40	,,
Edmond Humphrey	4	24	,,
James Morley .	1	17	,,
William Ford . .	1	1	pasture
	32	330	

All the convertible ground, except James Morley's, had appendant rights in the Rother meadows. Thomas Sacher and Richard Etherton controlled 12 acres of the first grass and 36 acres of the after-pasture of Wide Mead. John Bease and Edmond Humphrey shared the 3 acres of first grass in Mill Mead, and they, together with John Young and John Browne the 12 acres of first grass and 40 acres of after-pasture in Budham Mead.

[1] For these fields see maps XIIB and XIII.

The demesne leases were for twenty-one years and were renewed in 1577 and again in 1596/7. In 1577 the 8th Earl reduced the tenants to six instead of eight, while increasing the acreage to 384. Fortunately the original indentures for his relettings have been preserved:

1577

	Acres	*Rent* £	*s.*	*d.*
William Sacher . . .	96	19	5	0
Thomas Cranley and Thomas Humphrey . . .	50	10	2	8
John Browne . . .	52	10	9	0
Robert Ford . . .	99	19	17	0
William Edmond . .	45	9	1	0
John Ayer . . .	42	8	8	0
	384	£77	2	8

nearly 5*s.* an acre.

The recurrence of the names Sacher, Humphrey, Browne, and Ford may be noted. Robert Ford is described as 'Servant of the Earl'. In 1596/7 the 9th Earl carried through the second renewal for six tenants, again enlarging the acreage to 403 and raising the rent to £120:

1596/7

	Acres	*Rent* £	*s.*	*d.*
William Sacher. . .	121	36	10	0
Christopher Sacher . .	95	27	13	6
Thomas Libard . .	49	14	15	6
Elizabeth Ayer . .	48	14	8	0
William Heath . .	70	21	0	0
William Phillips[1] . .	20	6	0	0
	403	£120	7	0

nearly 6*s.* an acre.

The Sachers had now attained a commanding position.

The terms of both relettings are similar. Like copies of court rolls they reserved to the lord all timber, mine and

[1] Phillips was also bailiff of the manor. See below, p. 52.

quarry of stone with a right to enter the premises at any time to procure and carry away these products. The tenant was held responsible for repairing buildings, hedges, and ditches and had power to take house-, hedge-, and stake-bote for these purposes. He was forbidden to 'grind any grist or corn to be occupied or spent within the township of Petworth but only at the mill of the lord'. He was bound also by the following clause concerning his neighbours' rights of passage over the land as an open field:

> Provided always that it shall be lawful for other tenants of the demesne ground belonging to the site of the manor[1] to have free egress and regress for the carriage of corn, manure or soil from their lands with carts or other needful carriage through any part of the said demesne not sowed with corn standing or growing thereon as for neighbourhood heretofore hath been suffered and as often as need shall require.

The court, however, issued a contrary injunction in 1582 'that no tenant hereafter cross over the land of Robert Badger called Cookes or Peparams under heavy penalty of 10*s*. This protected area consisted of two closes, one on each side of Nightingale Lane.[2] No reason is given for the prohibition.

It is not possible to trace from one letting to another the various fields making up the different tenancies nor to locate the ground taken in at the renewals. The names given to many fields were not constant nor can fields always be identified by their acreages. There were many changes from one letting to another. New names appear without indicating their locality while old names drop out.

Of the thirty-two fields referred to in the 1557 survey seventeen are now part of the modern Frog Farm, the remaining fifteen being included in Soanes and Hoes

[1] The 'site of the manor' was the situation of the Manor House.

[2] See map XIIB, fields 27 and 35.

farms. In 1557 the seventeen were rented by six of the eight demesne tenants as shown below and in map XIIA:

	Fields	*Acres*	*Of his total of*
Thomas Sacher	1, 2, 17	43	89
Richard Etherton . . .	3, 4, 5, 6	30	66
Edmond Humphrey . .	11, 12, 13, 14	24	24
John Browne	7, 8	21	51
John Bease	15, 16	21	42
John Young	9, 10	12	40
			312
James Morley. . . .			17
William Ford . . .			1
	17	151	330

Each was a compact holding, except Thomas Sacher's no. 17. Sixty years later, in 1610,[1] the same area now including the 4½ acres of the football field was estimated to be 157 acres and was divided into twenty-five fields rented by nine tenants: but of them Robert Sadler of Cradlers in Upperton[2] was supreme, occupying nine fields: 1, 2, 3, 4, 6, 7, 8, 9, and 16—all contiguous except no. 6, and totalling 68 acres. In the plan for this year are also shown the fifteen fields into which the 53 acres lying outside the demesne area, but now included in Frog Farm, were divided between eleven owners. Number 26 was the Conduit Field, nos. 29, 38, and 40 were freeholds, nos. 37 and 39 were demesne. The remaining nine were copyholds in seven different hands.

One hundred and seventy years later a survey made by James Crowe shows the whole of Frog Farm as concentrated in the lord and let under the name of Pound Farm to one tenant, the Pound being in the north-east corner.[3] The farm's size also had been enlarged from 210 (157+53) to 225 acres mainly through the making in the 1760s of the present Petworth to Tillington road and by more accurate measurement. A few years later the present farm

[1] Map XIIB. [2] Below, pp. 91–92. [3] Map XIIC.

buildings were erected. The fields then numbered twenty-two. Today the farm has the same bounds but only ten subdivisions.[1]

North of Petworth the 1557 survey cites only parks and woods as being of the lord's demesne. The rest of the land, except the Lymes (29 acres)[2] and a few freehold tenements, was occupied by copyholders at fixed customary rents, having no relation to existing values and which inspired bitter complaints from the 9th Earl in his 'Discourse which concerneth Officers and Servants'. His father had initiated a steady policy of converting copyholds into demesne. He and all subsequent lords of the manor actively pursued it, much to the benefit of farming progress.

The 1557 survey gives a list of six woods with the estimated value of each per acre:

1. A common or 'outwood', that is, an unenclosed wood lying outside a park or demesne but the timber of which was a perquisite of the lord. Its area was 200 acres. It is now in the northern half of the present park. Being 'common' its enclosure into the park by the 9th Earl was opposed by the tenants of the manor in the court of Chancery.[3] In 1557 it contained beech and timber of 140 years growth, 'thin set', and worth 30*s.* an acre.

2. The Frith was particularly noted as 'the place where a goshawk breedeth'. The furnace of the ironworks was not yet established on its northern border but its 160 acres of 'most fair beach and some fair young timber oaks well set of 200 years growth' with the supplies of iron ore procurable from neighbouring copyholds and the available water supply made it appropriate to that enterprise. It was now valued at no more than 26*s.* 8*d.*

3. Colehook Wood (now Wet Wood and Russell Wood) had 76 acres of 'scrubbed oak and beach' 300 years old and worth only 20*s.*

4. Chawfold (Chaffold) Wood of 39 acres was the most

[1] Map XIID. [2] Map VIII. [3] Below, p. 59.

valuable of all with 'much fine timber some great beaches 220 years growth well set' and priced at 33*s*. 4*d*.

5. Ratfalling (Raffling) Wood, with 37 acres mostly beech of 180 years, was marked down at 18*s*. In 1571 it was described as a 'herbage wood'. John Byrymble, the bailiff and collector, was the tenant, and in it he had built a barn. In that year the Queen, who had then supplanted the 7th Earl as lord of the manor before his execution in 1572, renewed the lease for twenty-one years at a rent of 10*s*., reserving the valuable pannage season. Together with that of other demesne woods it was farmed at £40 a year.

6. Middlekorne was a wood in the twelfth century when Jocelyn de Louvain, after his marriage with Agnes the first Percy heiress, let pannage for five pigs in it on condition that the lessee erected a gate on the road to Ebernoe Common—a gate that was the direct ancestor of that at the point now called Streels Lane Gate.[1] In 1560, four centuries later, the court ordered James Louder to restore the gate and in consideration granted him pannage for five pigs and no more. The next year he was amerced for overgrazing. An antique post remained the sole relic of this ancient gate until a few years ago. In 1557 the 91 acres of Middlekorne Wood and the 'old scrubbed oaks and beaches some 240 years growth and thin set' were each worth 23*s*. 4*d*.[2]

Thus the value of the 603 acres of timber was £794. 6*s*. 2*d*. To this was added £81. 7*s*. 6*d*. for 108 acres of 'much fine young timber growing on the copyholds' and £240. 2*s*. for the trees in the hedgerows and in the 'common woods not measurable because they stood here and there straggling'. In them were 1,680 oaks and beeches, some of 300 years' growth of which 100 were 'fair timber trees' valued at 18*d*. a tree, bringing the total for all the timber to £1,115. 15*s*. 8*d*.

[1] Map VI. [2] For these Woods see maps XV, I, III, VI, VII.

Before 1610 many changes had occurred in these woods. The outwood of 200 acres had been enclosed into the park and Middlekorne Wood had become Middlecarr Common in circumstances which are described in this chapter. Against these losses the acreage of Colehook Wood had increased to 108 and that of Raffling Wood to 97. In the result, omitting the outwood, the increases more than balanced the losses:

	1557	*1610*
The Frith	160	171
Colehook	75	108
Chaffold	39	37
Raffling	37	97
Middlekorne	91	..
	402	413

The addition to Colehook appears to have been new planting. The enlargement of Raffling Wood was due to the addition to it of a part of the Guntersbridge copyhold[1] which the 8th Earl bought from John Heath and thus converted to demesne. On this point a lease of June 1596 to William Phillips the bailiff is suggestive. It demised the pasture and wood called Ratfalling Wood 'with the several closes as they be now enclosed of arable and pasture appertaining to the wood . . . excepting the great woods growing and all the quarries'. The phrase 'the several closes as they be now enclosed' implies taken into the wood. All the agricultural part of the farm was let to John Mose. In 1610 some of the trees in the wood are said to be of thirty years' growth. When Chilnhurst (Chillinghurst)[2] was acquired about another hundred acres of enclosed wood were added to the total.

The 1557 survey omits Idehurst from the list of demesne land and woods. Its situation is clearly shown on the 1610 map in relation to the Rectory Brook and the buildings of Shimmins Farm.[3] It is mentioned in the

[1] Map VIII and below, p. 107.

[2] Map XV.

[3] Map XVI.

Percy Chartulary as having been granted to Eleanore, widow of Henry, 9th Baron de Percy, towards the end of the thirteenth century. It was then said to be $55\frac{1}{2}$ acres with 2 acres each of garden, of wood, and of Wide Mead. The 1610 map gives it 75 acres and shows it to be an enclosed rough pasture with a barn and a road passing diagonally across it from south-west to north-east closed by a gate at each end. Most of the timber on it had been cut and used in building the famous stables that Defoe admired so much. But the map shows two plantations still standing; and when the 9th Earl came out of the Tower he got the consent of Dr. Bownde, 'the painful pastor' of Petworth, to open a way for carts to cross the glebe to the parsonage, thus enabling timber and charcoal to be brought direct from Idehurst and Flexham Park. The alternative route, used for the timber to build the stables, and at least half a mile longer, was through the southern Idehurst gate, 'between Bowyer's[1] meads' into the Little Leith to the Byworth road. Barton's Lane did not then exist. Only a stile led to a footpath over the glebe. With Dr. Bownde's consent a gate was now added. Unfortunately an accident occurred which caused the road to be closed, though the gate remained. The story was told by John Parker at an inquiry held in July 1677, when he was aged eighty-one:

He remembers when there was so much wood within the Parsonage lands of Petworth that a cart could not go from the Idehurst. That afterwards, when a way was made for a cart, coles of the Earle of Northumberland was brought from there by the permission of Dr. Bownde for that when a load was brought down one William Satcher went to the parsonage house to borrow the keys to pass the gate whilst William Gale stole some cole brands out of the cart which he hid in the stall among the straw, they took fire and burnt down the barn. And

[1] This was Ralph Bowyer, the owner of Kitts in East Street and three freeholds near Hungers Lane. Map XIIB. Fields K, N, R.

that where the gate to the Idehurst now is was no other than a stile.

After 1617 the importance of Idehurst was much increased by the 9th Earl's purchase of the Earl of Northampton's moiety of the manor of Byworth[1] followed by his acquisition of the other moiety from Sir Henry Goring in 1620. This latter transaction was curiously connected with the founding of Thomas Thompson's almshouses in North Street for twelve poor persons of either sex, inhabitants of Petworth. Thomas Thompson of Barnards Inn in Holborn, London, died in December 1618 having in the previous May advanced Sir Henry Goring £730 on the security of his moiety of the Byworth Manor. In his will he left this moiety as one of the endowments of his prospective almshouses on the condition that if Sir Henry repaid the £730 the moiety was to be released to him. The 9th Earl now stepped in and for £800 got the property conveyed to himself. Furthermore for £430 he acquired from Goring seven small freeholds, nine copyhold farms, and Baynard's Wood totalling upwards of 500 acres, as well as Brinksole Heath, Egdean Common, and Egdean Fair. A good bargain for the Earl.

The existence of the gate next the stile naturally encouraged a belief that it opened on to a way for carts as the stile did for pedestrians. At the general court held on 12 September 1654 the homage insisted that there was 'such a usual way . . . constantly used without any contradiction'. In support they produced a declaration by Nicholas Morris 'aged about four score' that 'three score years ago' the trees on Idehurst had been felled and 'carried up through the parsonage wood and gate in carts'. He went on to declare that the lord of the manor 'ought to have free passage for carts, carriages or otherwise'. His statement that the road was opened threescore years ago

[1] This purchase, by including Lord Northampton's demesne, rounded off the demesne of Petworth. Map XIII.

implies the date 1594, On the other hand, the witnesses before a second inquiry held in 1677 agree that the gate beside the stile was erected after the 9th Earl came out of the Tower. Thus Peter Bowyer testified that he knew no gate before then and that the Earl of Northumberland's way from Idehurst was 'between Bowyer's meads into the Little Lyth'. He remembered as a boy helping with three of the Earl's teams in transporting timber to be used in building the stables and always using the Byworth road. It was half a mile longer than the direct way through the glebe, but it was 'more commodious for that heavy carriage'. Two other witnesses confirmed his evidence. In the end the Duke of Somerset established his own right of way after he had become lord of the manor of Petworth Rectory.

Coming next to the parks. There were three:

The Coney Park or Conyngere or Conygre.
The Middle or Little Park.
The Michel or Great Park.

The Coney Park was described in the time of William, 8th Baron de Percy (1193–1245) as 'the new small park in which is his cunegeria'. During his lifetime he added more than a hide of land to it by means of exchanges. His grandson Henry, 10th Baron, followed his example by exchanging 17½ acres.[1] No doubt these accretions formed part of the Middle Park to which the 5th Earl of Northumberland in 1499, the year in which he came of age, added 105 acres more. Among them were John Sturt's copyhold of 15 acres of arable land lying 'direct against the Conygre' and a freehold tenement of 25 acres. In 1539 Thomas Aylwyn was presented for having built a cottage on land near Upperton 'next the Little Park'. The difficulty of computing the total acreage of these imparkings is the absence of information on the acreage covered by the term 'hide'.

[1] Percy Chartulary 407, 409, 415, 417, 441.

The Survey of 1557 confirms the three parks and calls the Middle Park the Little Park:

There is three parks belonging to the Honour of Petworth (that is to say) the Coney Park, the Little Park and the Great Park which hath much good timber and wood in them; and the furthest which is four miles from Petworth which is the Great Park and the other but one mile wherein the mansion house standeth[1] and also a lodge for a keeper which is partly decayed. . . . Also there is in the same park a commodious piece of ground enclosed with a pale called the Arbour Hill which hath in it divers pleasant walks divided with quickset hedge used to be cut. Moreover there is in the same park divers burrows with coneys and a fair large pond for fish. It is reasonably replenished with fair timber oaks and hath in it at present about the number of [blank] deer. Moreover there was lately taken into the said park within these fifteen years divers small closes containing by estimation 12 acres which was most commonly used for arable ground and for that by enclosing the same the Parson of Petworth[2] wanteth the tythe of corn he was wont to have. He hath made petition to the Commissioners for reasonable yearly allowance to be made to him in recompence for the same and we esteem 21s 6d for it.

The description of Arbour Hill as enclosed with a pale and decked with pleasant walks and quickset hedges shows that these amenities had been added to it while the manor was in the hands of the Crown; and apparently without obtaining the consent of the homage. Hence the 7th Earl found it necessary to apply to the court for this consent on 15 September 1558. And this was granted in the following resolution:

ffor Inclosynge the Herber Hyll ynto ye Conyngar

That the tenaunts of this manor at the Court holden there the day and yere above wrytten for them and theyre heyres Do

[1] The one mile must refer to the northern boundary of the park.

[2] The Rev. Thomas Mandeville, who had claimed heriots on descents and alienations of free tenements.

frely graunt unto the wryght honorable Erle of Northumberland that hit shalbe lawfull for the sayde Erle Lord of this manor at all tyme and tymes hereafter at his and theyre will and pleasure to take Inne, Inclose and Imparke ynto his parke called the Conyngar one parcell of the comon unto the sayde parke adioynyng. That is to say from the north gate comonly called the comon parke gate unto the upper Berewell as the grene waye leadethe from the sayde parke gate comonly called the comon gate runnyng uppe towards upper Bearewell aforesayde and as the grene waye leadeth on the west part of the herber hill wiche comon dothe conteyne by estimacion tenne akers be hit more or lesse so as the graunting thereof from henceforthe may not be preiudyciall unto their olde auncyent customes. In the presence of Sir Thomas Palmer Knight, William Dawtrey esquyre and John Dudley gentylmon with dyverse others.

The consent of the homage was necessary as enclosing Arbour Hill into the Coney Park deprived the tenants of their commonable rights over it. The green way west of the hill is the valley between it and Snowhill. The north gate presumably was in the fence of the Coney Park. Thus Arbour Hill became an enclave of that park surrounded on three sides by the Little Park over which the tenants reserved their rights.[1]

The statement that the Little Park was 'but one mile from Petworth' is contradicted by the addition 'wherein the mansion house standeth'. It contained also 'a fair large pond' on part of the ground covered by the present upper pond but not more than a third of its size. In 1564 more deer were added to its rabbits. They were caught in the Great Park by a toyle costing £8. 16*s*. 6*d*., and to protect them a custodian was appointed at a salary of £3. 0*s*. 10*d*. At the same time £13. 19*s*. 8*d*. was spent on the pale.

Another account of the parks in 1557 suggested disparking them and letting the land at rack rents. The

[1] Map XV.

amenities of Arbour Hill are not mentioned in this document, but it contains estimates of the deer and rabbit populations. In the Coneygarth there were 'of all sorts of deer by estimation 60 and 200 couple of conies'. Its acreage was calculated at 80 'with much fine timber therein'. Disparked it could be let for £13. 6*s.* 8*d.* or 3*s.* 4*d.* an acre. The Little Park was said to measure as much as 300 acres (certainly an overstatement), being 'well set with beaches and oaks', and with 200 deer of all sorts and 300 couple of conies. It was, however, the barrenest of the parks and its rental after disparking was estimated at no more than £20 or 1*s.* 4*d.* an acre. The Great Park was given only 400 acres[1] with 140 deer and no conies, and 'but thinly set with oaks and beaches'. Its soil being somewhat better than that of the Little Park the suggested rental was £33. 6*s.* 8*d.* or 1*s.* 8*d.* an acre. This disparking proposal was not adopted. But the Great Park became demesne farm land sixty years later.

In 1610 the mansion house and its policies occupied the same 6 acres as they did in 1557. But the Birchen Walks of 8½ acres had been added to them at the expense of the Conygre. The Little Park had become the Home Park, and its acreage was reduced to 187. It now had a fence called the Five Rails Fence along the northern boundary, passing from Snowhill just north of Arbour Hill to the park pale on the London Way. This fence was one of the causes for the long dispute between the 9th Earl and his tenants. Another was his action in enclosing the 'outwood'.[2]

Under the statute of Merton the lord could enclose waste or common provided he left sufficient for the tenants, a point on which he could procure the consent of the homage as did the 7th Earl, or he could consult with and come to terms with the tenants. An example of con-

[1] In 1610 the Great Park acreage is stated to be 691. See below, p. 64.

[2] The land on which Thomas Aylwyn built his cottage was said to be a 'parcel of the Common of Petworth'.

sultation was the order issued by Richard Stokes, the sub-seneschal, to the Messor:

These are to will you to signify William Goble shoemaker that the Lord of the Honour is to build and make tenements upon the waste betwixt the gutter[1] and the tenement of the said Goble in the town of Petworth. If therefore the said Goble or any of his friends and co-tenants can shew any deeds or evidence to claim any part of the foresaid waste and shew sufficient matter at the next court holden for ye Lord of the said Honour on Friday being the 25th day of this present month of July then and there it shall be ordered as shall appear. And also that the said Goble bring then with him the deeds and [writings?] of his free land and to shew by what right he built the barn now standing in the said town.

Fail you not. Dated at Petworth July 15 1609 by me
Richard Stokes. Seneschal.

In order to secure the consent of the tenants to the Five Rails Fence the 8th Earl granted them the pannage of the 91 acres of Middlekorne Wood, afterwards Middlecarr, and now Colehook, Common. But hostility to this arrangement revived when the 9th Earl proposed to impark the 200 acres of the outwood. The scenes of violence that followed are described in a letter he wrote to Sir John Pickering, the lord keeper, on 19 July 1592 after the copyholders had carried their case to the court of Chancery:[2]

They (the tenants) have oftsoons renewed their secret and riotous pulling down in the night season by themselves and accomplices my pales and enclosures, as well of those lands in question before the Chancery (whereof my father and self have had quiet possession by the space of sixteen years or thereabouts) as of my own freeholds and demesne no whit touched by the said controversy.

[1] The gutter was a surface drain running down the Causey (now Lombard Street) across Market Place to Sowter (now Pound) Street. William Goble held a free tenement in the Market and another in Sowter Street near Hog Lane.

[2] De Fonblanque, i. 195–6.

They had even cut the connexion between Petworth House and the local water supply. He was anxious that the lord keeper should know of these outrages in coming to his decision.

In their bill of complaint the copyholders denied that they had agreed to accept the pannage in exchange for the Five Rails Fence. They roundly claimed that both the grazing of the park and the pannage of Middlekorne were theirs already by custom and that in any event the pannage was worth no more than 40*s.* a year. Furthermore they asserted that three or four years after the enclosure the 8th Earl had felled all the trees and so had destroyed whatever pannage there was. This was unquestionably true, for in 1610 Middlekorne had ceased to be a wood and was now Middlecarr Common. In his rejoinder the 9th Earl produced evidence that the annual value of the grazing enclosed by the Five Rails Fence was no more than 5 nobles (£1. 13*s.* 4*d.*), whereas the pannage had been worth as much as £40 since the tenants had had it. He seems to have exaggerated here, for £40 was the rent of the pannage of all demesne woods let for the purpose and not for Middlekorne alone. He was able to claim, however, that the felling of the trees of Middlekorne had so far improved its pasture as to make it a sufficient countervail for the outwood and the Five Rails Fence.

The law action in Chancery now continued its leisurely course, and in November 1594 the Earl was more conciliatory. He was willing, he wrote to the lord keeper, to deal with the objectors better than they deserved. Nevertheless, until their minds were altered as touching their supposed wrongs, he saw no hope of them taking anything thankfully from him. He prayed the lord keeper therefore to continue hearing their complaints, and when these were exhausted he would show more regard for the tenants than they deserved, considering their clamours.[1]

[1] De Fonblanque, i. 196–7.

A year later he agreed to commissioners being appointed to examine what the annual value of the pannage of Middlekorne was before the enclosure and the present value of its pasture. But he objected to any inquiry into the erection of the Five Rails Fence. Moreover, he was so confident of his right in the matter of the outwood that he let the ground in 1595 to Thomas Kelton, a gentleman of Petworth, for twenty-one years. The rent was no more than £5, but Kelton was required within the first three years of his lease to subdivide the area at his own cost with quickset hedges and with ditches, and to clear it of bushes, hollies, and shrubs 'for the better augmenting and saving of the Spring and incoppizing thereof'—that is to say, the trees were to be planted as a copse for periodical cutting, not for mature timber. Thereafter he had to preserve the ground 'from the outrage and annoying of any cattle', including his own. He was allowed gate- and hedge-bote for the enclosures, and he had a house in the park. The only evidence that he carried out his obligations were two plantations near the London Way, one 'sowed with acorns' and the other marked 'enclosed wood'. There is no wood on their sites today.[1]

Despite the Earl's objection the court of Chancery insisted on inquiring into the land enclosed by the Five Rails Fence and issued a decree giving the following instructions to Commissioners:

1. To survey the enclosure and the waste ground left for the tenants to common.
2. To report on the value of the common before the enclosure.
3. To report on the value of the ground now enclosed which was before common.
4. To report on the cost of impaling, enclosing, grubbing and bettering the enclosed land and the consequent increase in its value.

[1] Map XV.

5. To estimate the value of the pannage of Middlekorne before the trees were felled.
6. To judge whether the same ground without the trees was of better value and if so how much.
7. To enquire whether the tenants now had sufficient common.
8. To state what ways or passages they should have to the places where they have common.
9. To declare whether they have been sufficiently recompensed by the pannage or by the bettering of the pasture of Middlekorne by the felling of the trees.

The Commissioners' report is not available, but a declaration addressed to the Earl and signed by 102 of his tenants, including 22 of the 49 who organized the bill of complaint, shows that a satisfactory settlement was made. In it they, on behalf of the whole company of his tenants, assured him:

that whereas of late years by reason of some suites and controversies in the law made and commenced by us against Your Honour we have worthily drawn upon ourselves Your Honour's disfavour, we are most heartily sorry for the same and by these our letter of submission do most humbly crave pardon thereof at Your Honour's hands, promising and protesting that at all times hereafter we shall and will (God's Grace so assisting us) in all things and by all means shew and demesne ourselves as loyal and dutiful tenants unto Your Honour. And as touching the matter now in controversy and as yet in law depending, for the more speedy determining and ending of the same, we do willingly and with one assent refer them wholly unto Your Honour's hands assuring ourselves that (according to your honourable disposition unto pity and compassion towards all) Your Honour will give and take such favourable regard for us your poor tenants in our distressed estate as that thereby we shall remain most bounden every one of us, our wives, children and posterity in succeeding ages to pray daily to Almighty God for Your Honour and all yours to whose Grace and protection with our hands to this submission jointly subscribed and our hearts to His Heavenly

Majesty lifted up we humbly now and ever remain Your Good Honour's dutiful tenants.

Three tenants dissociated themselves entirely from any connexion with the court proceedings. John Edsall of Foxbeeches near Upperton 'did disclaim from winning in the suit and did willingly submit himself to My Lord'. Robert Sadler of Upperton and Henry Beech, tenant of a shop and cellar in Market Place, were 'never partakers in the suit'.[1]

The park now spread rapidly northwards, and in 1610 another addition called 'the New Park' appears. Its acreage is entered in the terrier as 821.[2] That it was new and had a substantial lodge in it are testimonies to the improving zeal of the 9th Earl. No compensation seems to have been due to the tenants for its imparking. No Pheasant Copse then existed. Three little copyhold cottages still lingered within its precincts. The two plantations, one marked 'sowed with acorns' and the other 'enclosed wood', may be accepted as the first steps towards its creation. That acorns had to be sown was one of the complaints of the 9th Earl in his 'Discourse which concerneth Officers and Servants' addressed to his son:

Instead of preserving woods that might easily have been raised, the memory of good trees in rotten roots doth appear above ground at this day; being forced now for the fuel relief of your house at Petworth to sow acorns, whereas I might have had plenty if either they had had care or I knowledge.

He was pessimistic about his son's supply of fuel for Petworth House. Fuel wood was sold by the cord, a stack pile 8×4×4 ft. During the seven years 1594–1600 an annual average of 1,030 cords was sold: not, it would seem, a very large quantity for so well wooded a neighbourhood. But the Earl's complaint was of a failure to

[1] For Foxbeeches and Robert Sadler see map X. For Henry Beech see below, p. 126.

[2] The 1610 map states the acreage as 794.

replant. The Pheasant Copse was a result of his anxiety on this point. It owed its name to the 9th and 10th Earls' interest in pheasants. Accounts contain frequent references to their luxurious feeding, and the yard to which the gate of the manor gave entrance was called the Pheasant Yard

Beyond the area of the Pheasant Copse the New Park did not then stretch as far north as Stag Park does now. Its northern pale started from just beyond the third mile post from Petworth. It then passed south of the modern Lodgefield Copse and, excluding Chillinghurst, joined the western boundary at White's Green where Thomas White lived.[1] There was no junction between this northern section and the ancient Great or Michel Park which was more than four miles from Petworth stretching eastward from the Frith and Colehook Wood. Beyond it was Frithfold, the modern Upper Frithfold Farm. The pale of the Michel Park did not enclose Frithfold, but the two were included in the 804 acres of the park:[2]

	Arable	*Pasture*	*Total*
Frithfold . . .	39	74	113
The Great Park .	312	379	691
	351	453	804

The arable of Frithfold was separated from the pasture by a division still marked by an existing fence. A barn in the north-west corner was the only building on Frithfold. Nearby was a cottage of which in 1610 Robert Ashlott was the customary tenant at a rent of 2*s*. In 1635 Edward Piper became the copyholder and gave his name to the present Pipers Cottages and the adjoining Pipers Copse. The herbage of Frithfold was let at £17. One huge 'woody piece of ground' occupied 61 acres of it, an area now harnessed into nine convenient fields.

The Great Park was no longer classified as a park in

[1] Map XV.

[2] Map II.

1610 though it still retained that name. It was now listed as demesne farm land with an isolated house in the north-west corner be sides the many buildings connected with the iron industry.[1] The establishment of these works before 1572 was the first stage in the conversion of the park. The hammer then became its central feature with the furnace on the northern border of the Frith. These brought in a rent of £100, while the grazing was leased in 1593 to Samuel Britton of North Street, Petworth, for twenty-one years at £60 a year. When this lease ended the second stage began with Sir Edward Francis becoming the tenant for a like term in consideration of a sum of £1,400. The lease specially empowered him: to divide and enclose the park as he 'should think meet and convenient for his better manurance, profit and husbandry'; to rid it of furze and other annoyances and 'to cleanse and dig it to his best commodity and advantage'. The 1610 map shows that much in these directions had already been done before he took over, but at the end of this term the land was ripe to be let to ten tenants for £265. 2*s.* 6*d.*, or about 6*s.* 5*d.* an acre, a high rent. Ten years later, however, an abatement of 25 per cent. was necessary, to £199, or 4*s.* 10*d.* an acre.

The expansion of the park was accompanied by an equally notable enlargement of the demesne. We have already noted the acquisition of Guntersbridge. The purchases of Osettes or Osiers, of Ashfold, Laces, and Uplands are dealt with in Chapter 4. In order to reach the total they are included in the acreage list below with Guntersbridge and the other tenements which were to the north of the park and were now or later taken into it. All were compact tenements. Guntersbridge, apart from Raffling Wood, was now a demesne farm rented to John Mose, an energetic man who co-operated with the Earl in enlarging the park and who for eight years was active

[1] Below, Chap. 5.

in the iron trade. His lease was for twenty-one years at a rent of £24, or 3*s.* 8*d.* an acre. Under him land that had never been ploughed produced crops of oats encouraged by a plan requiring rents to be paid in grain.[1] Buttyns is described in the terrier as 'demesne at Copthurst and Buttyns purchased of Shude'. The only place on the map into which it can fit is the north-east corner of the park. Imparking seems to have robbed it of its identity.[2]

	Arable	*Pasture*	*Meadow*	*Woods*	*Total*
Guntersbridge	..	95	35	53	183
Osiers	32	38	..	..	70
Ashfold	..	22	..	..	22
Laces	8	20	2	..	30
Uplands	12	27	5	9	53
Buttyns	..	51	..	..	51
Bishops 1	23	16	1	3	43
Bishops 2	31	2	..	16	49
Chillinghurst	53	73	..	100	226
North Parkhurst	32	10	..	..	42
South Parkhurst	15½	25½	..	..	41
	206½	379½	43	181	810

Bishops 1 and North Parkhurst were in 1606 occupied by William Derrick and his wife as life tenants by her right, the reversion being to Judith Rooke and her son. When Judith died her son sold the reversion to John Mose who transferred it to the 9th Earl. Mose then secured a twenty-one years' lease of the land (renewable every seventh year) from the Derricks and passed that also to the Earl, who thus obtained immediate possession for all time unless one of the Derricks lived for more than twenty-one years—an unlikely contingency that did not occur. North Parkhurst is not marked on the map, but the terrier's description of it shows clearly its location. Two of its closes adjoined the houses of John and Roger Jackson and Henry Stent, situated on the site of the

[1] See Chap. 5.

[2] Map XV.

present Jackson's Lodge.[1] Another was 'where the gate standeth' as shown on map XV. Two others were 'next the brook' and 'next the Lane' from Copthurst to Chilnhurst. Bishops 2 was sold to the Earl by Richard Goble. Chilnhurst was held of the Lord Montagu's manor of River at a rent of £1. It was sold to the Earl by John Bonner of Shillinglee. At the southern point of its triangular shape stood the cottage of Thomas White, whose name survives in White's Green. The terrier classifies its 225 acres as:

Arable	53
Pasture	72
Wood	100[2]
	225

The first demesne tenant was John Dench who got it on a year-to-year lease at a rent of £26. Assuming that he took the 125 acres of arable and pasture the rent was equivalent to about 4*s.* 6*d.* an acre. South Parkhurst belongs to a different group of farms dealt with hereafter. The terrier declares that it was 'purchased of Person Dyrig'. This being interpreted would appear to mean a person named Derrick, or William Derrick.

[1] The grandsons of the two Jacksons mortgaged the houses, with the result that both passed to the lord of the manor. The Stent cottage was bought by the Duke of Somerset in 1697.

[2] The terrier enters arable as 100 acres and woods as 53 acres. The map discloses this error.

4

THE COPYHOLDS

IN this chapter we propose to pay calls on some of the copyholds in the northern half of the manor, remarking on their histories and their tenants.

The first to be visited must be Nicholas Alderton's three copyholds: Sibbs and Little Sibbs, Hambledens, and Redhill lying to the east of Osiers. They were only a part of Alderton's estate which as a whole consisted of:

	Arable	*Pasture*	*Meadow*	*Total Acreage*	*Rent*
1. Sibbs and Little Sibbs .	18	19	..	37	6*s*. 4*d*.
2. Hambledens . . .	15	3	..	18	2*s*. 10*d*.
3. Redhill	3	7	8	18	6*s*. 4*d*.
4. Furtherlees near Guntersbridge with a house on it	15	6	..	21	6*s*. 0*d*.
5. The Bakehouse near the cemetery . . .	..	..	..	..	2*d*.
6. Inholmes . . .	3	..	..	3	3*s*. 6*d*.
7. Holebroke Mead . .	..	..	4	4	4*s*. 0*d*.
8. Beales and Bridgemead at Rotherbridge with fishery	2	7	2	11	13*s*. 8*d*.
	56	42	14	112	42*s*. 10*d*.

He was the freeholder also of meadow land to the north of Upper and Budham Meads, and he owned as well two parcels in Budham Mead.[1]

On his father's death his mother had taken all as her bench except Sibbs, Hambledens, and Redhill. These had come in 1571 direct to Thomas the youngest of her sons and his father's heir, he being then aged two. Next year

[1] These parcels were nos. 19 and 55 in map XIVB. For Sibbs, Little Sibbs, Hambledens, and Redhill see map VII; for Furtherlees map VIII; for Inholmes map XIIB; for Holbroke Mead, Beales, and Bridgemead map XIII.

he had died and Nicholas his elder brother aged seven had replaced him. When he in turn came of age in 1586 his mother, with the co-operation of her second husband Thomas Cranley, one of the demesne tenants, surrendered Furtherlees, Holebroke Mead, and Beales and Bridgemead to him. He was thus more amply endowed than his father had been. Nor was his estate so awkward to manage as might at first sight appear. Of the 56 acres of arable 51 were connected by the Kirdford Way. The house in Furtherlees was well placed as a headquarters —more convenient than the Bakehouse. Moreover, Nicholas, unlike his son Henry, who was Reeve for seventeen years, served the manor only once, as a messor. He was a farmer. The extent of his operations and the value of his freehold meadow land may be gathered from the heriots seized after his death in 1616. For his nine copyholds six cows and three heifers were taken.

His widow Mary had all as her bench as well as the guardianship of Thomas her youngest son and heir, then aged eleven. Under him when of age the estate was dispersed.

In 1627 Holebroke Mead passed to Edward Pellett, aged seven, who disposed of it as soon as he could. Furtherlees and Inholmes became the property of Richard Yates the Bailiff who later sold them to Nicholas Smart, the butcher, and his son.[1] The Bakehouse fell to Edmund Springall, whose standard of living can be gauged by the inventory of his chattels when he was in debt:

> One feather bed, one bolster and a pillow weight 72 lbs; one flock bed weight 36 lbs; one green rug and a cover lid; four quisions and a chair; five curtains and a blanket; one cupboard and a table; a testament and an old silver bodkin and other things in a purse; a psalm book; three napkins and a pillow-bere; fourteen napkins, seven old bands; a silk garter; three old sheets, fifteen small cloths, five long towels, four pillow-beres, a pair of satin sleeves; an old trunk.

[1] See p. 112.

He managed temporarily to save the situation by a mortgage to Nicholas Smart—until Nicholas foreclosed and so added the Bakehouse to his other Alderton acquisitions. In 1632 Thomas mortgaged Beales and Bridgemead to his brother Henry for £130. Henry, when he foreclosed, settled them on his infant son Richard. When Richard got possession after his mother's death he raised £100 on them and had in consequence to surrender them to his mortgagee five years later.

The history of Sibbs, Hambledens, and Redhill is of a successful mortgage. Thomas Alderton transferred them in 1634 to his brother William, who occupied them for forty-two years until his death in 1676. His son and heir William died ten years later.[1] Thereafter the premises passed to James South, a neighbour at Keyfox and Stanbridge, near Petworth Common, whose son was a successful mortgagor. In 1708 he raised £100 on Stanbridge[2] and £200 on Sibbs, Hambledens, and Redhill. He redeemed Stanbridge on the due date, and, after two renewals of the liability on the other three and raising the amount to £300, he paid that off also.

[1]

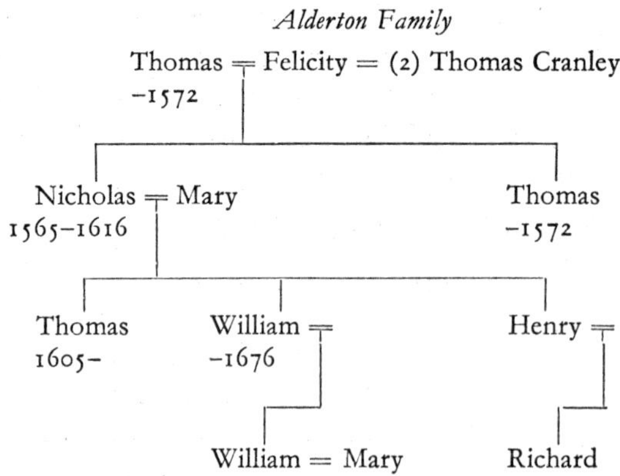

[2] Stanbridge is described as 'three customary closes near Petworth Common' of 12 acres more or less. This points to its being the tenement marked Anthony Finch in map VIII, though the acreage is there stated to be nearly 14.

The adjoining copyhold to the west was Ossettes or Osserts (now Osiers)[1] of 70 acres, 38 arable and 32 pasture. The year after his release from the Tower the 9th Earl bought it in interesting circumstances. In Elizabeth's reign it was held by Thomas Dench, whose widow Margaret died as its bencher in 1605. She had had three husbands. The first was Older of Rutlington,[2] by whom she had a son Richard. The second was Thomas Dench, the father of her son Robert. The third was Peter Young. Her Dench son Robert was nine when she died and her Older son Richard was appointed his guardian, being correctly described as 'brother on the mother's side of the said Robert'. Ten years later he and his ward, then aged nineteen, made an agreement ending the guardianship. A ward on reaching the age of fourteen could release his guardian by agreement with him and appoint another. As Robert died soon afterwards none other was required. The terms on which they parted were:

1. That Robert should have the profits of the copyhold at once and 'presently two suits of apparel'.
2. That he should have liberty to dispose of himself and of his estate at his pleasure.
3. That his guardian should be discharged 'of and from all troubles and reparations that might arise concerning the guardianship'.

After Robert's death his half-brother and late guardian Richard was admitted and surrendered the property to the lord for £150.[3] It seems wrong that Richard should have been Robert's guardian if he was to be his heir. As a demesne farm Osiers was let to Henry Holland at a rent of £18 or 12 per cent. on the purchase price and a return of 5*s*. an acre. The ancient rent was 8*s*. 9*d*. Under the new

[1] Map VII.
[2] Now Ridlington Farm in Duncton parish.
[3] See the transfer between two stepbrothers recorded on p. 87.

control the farm became the most reliable producer of oats.[1]

Robert Willard was admitted in 1571 to the 23 acres of the adjoining tenement called Horseberries[2] which had only 5 acres of arable. His family retained possession for the next century until in 1673 Henry Willard parted with it to William Hampton, whose son Thomas succeeded him in 1710.

The next copyholder on the list was William Miles. He occupied two tenements, both predominantly pastoral, the largest close in each being 'woody' inferior pasture:

	Arable	*Pasture*	*Meadow*	*Total*
Redhill[3] . .	6	25	3	34
Blackwool .	6	17	2	25
	12	42	5	59

He had made good his claim to Redhill in 1605 by producing a copy of a lost court roll. He died in 1640 and was succeeded by his son John, who shared the contemporary urge for improvement. He first mortgaged Redhill for £60 to William Hardham, who was tenant of the house in Petworth previously occupied by Henry Trashe the musician. He then raised £70 on Blackwool from Leonard Rooke. The first liability caused the loss of the property, for Hardham foreclosed and sold it to Anthony Sowter, he who had been made responsible for the education of Richard Boxall of Wisdoms. He raised the purchase price of £60 by a mortgage to Rooke. Miles successfully redeemed Blackwool and when he died in October 1649 his widow Anne was able to enter it as her bench, free of the encumbrance. By John she had had three surviving sons: John, William, and Nicholas. Nicholas, the youngest, was the customary heir, but his elder brother William, coveting the inheritance, murdered him.

[1] See Chap. 5. [2] Map VII. [3] Map VII.

He then attempted a rapid evasion of the consequences by surrendering Blackwool to Elizabeth Combes[1] of Northchapel at the court held on 27 October 1657 immediately following that at which his mother's death had been presented. But the customary three proclamations involved at least six weeks' delay, and within that time his fate was sealed. The inevitable result followed:

> A seizure at this court is awarded of the copyhold lands of William Miles in Northchapel called Blackwoolls into the hands of the Lord of this Manor and the Bayliffe to render an account to the Lord of the profits thereof.

Thus escheated the farm remained at the lord's disposal until 14 December 1658. John Miles then applied for it and was admitted by the grace of the lord on the substantial fine of £40. When he surrendered it two years later to John Pennicod the fine was £20.

Knightleys,[2] the copyhold north of Blackwool, was tenanted by William Boyes until his death in 1640. His widow died a year later leaving her son Anthony, then aged ten, under the guardianship of Joan Puttock. Knightleys was of 32 acres: arable 18, pasture 9½, and meadow 4½. These details are needed, as Anthony, when he was able to start mortgaging in 1651, began by pledging his 14 acres of pasture and meadow as security for a loan of £60. Thereafter his descent was rapid. A year and a half later he pledged the 18 acres of arable for £40. After six months he raised £20 more on the arable: and in 1657 and 1658 £140 more, making in all £260, equal to £8 an acre. The liquidation of this large sum involved the property passing to another.

These three copyholds: Redhill, Blackwool, and Knightleys were on the eastern border of the manor. Close to them, on the London Way, opposite the most northerly gate of the park, was a lonely cottage and

[1] Why to Elizabeth Combes is a mystery.
[2] Maps VI and VII.

garden where Henry Goodier lived rent free.[1] The site had been granted to him by the lord at the Michaelmas Court in 1606 'with the assent of many customary tenants' so that he might build a habitation for himself. Later his abode was replaced by the Greyhound Ale House which in turn has passed away. A similar isolated abode rent free was widow Shertowe's in the centre of the cross-shaped Middlecarr Common.[2] In 1610 it had no garden, a defect remedied before 1779 when Elizabeth Keene was the tenant.

From this point, looking eastward towards Jocelyn de Louvain's gate, the surveyor had on his right hand John Stent's Little London copyhold where Little London is today. Behind him was Parks, a part of John Stent's farm. On his left was a greater variety of ownerships. Nearest the gate was Edward Rawson's copyhold called Sabins, of 14 acres with a cottage, barn, and orchard. He had been admitted to it in 1605, as also to another barn and an adjacent parcel of land. The heriots and fines on both appear to have been fixed by custom. Two other cottages were neighbours. On the same site there are now seven habitations.[3]

Next to Edward Rawson was John Shude or Shudd,[4] whose house was on the same site as the present Colehook Farm steading. Of his 52 acres, of which 32½ were arable, 21 called Kechners lay east of the common and 31 called Brinckfold west of it. Adjoining to the south was half of Boxall's Wisdoms, whose history was touched on in the first chapter. This portion and Brinckfold, Kechners, and Sabins now together constitute Colehook Farm, the outer boundaries being still as they were in 1610. The remainder of the land on the north side of the common was dominated by John Stent's Sweetlands, except where this was bisected by the other part of Wisdoms and by an

[1] Map VII. [2] Map VI. [3] Map. VI.

[4] Perhaps the same man as the seller of Buttyns.

intrusion of Thomas Andrews's 88 acres stretching northwards towards Northchapel. Sweetlands farmstead was on the London Way; and the land overflowed the Way to where John Stent's brother William was the copyholder of the 52 acres of Knowles.[1]

The Stent family pedigree may be suggested as follows:

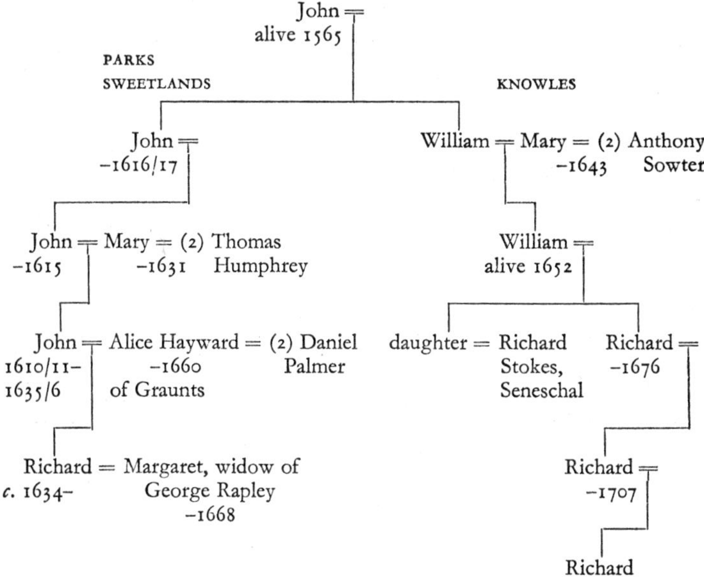

John Stent of Sweetlands and Parks, seeing his end approaching in 1615, began to surrender his estate. He sold the Ashfold portion of Sweetlands to the 9th Earl. Its 21 acres were equally divided between a coppice of birch of twenty-five years' growth and a pasture. The Earl reserved the coppice as an enclosed wood in his own hands. He let the pasture for twenty-one years at a rent of £6, say 5*s*. 9*d*. an acre, compared with the ancient copyhold rent of 17*s*. 4*d*. for the entire 81 acres of Sweetlands. Ashfold copse still retains its bounds of 1610, but it has been extended to the south beyond its former limits.[2]

[1] Maps VI and XV. [2] Map VI.

John's second surrender, including the rest of Sweetlands with the farm house on the London Way, was to his son John. John, however, died a year later leaving his widow Mary and an infant son John aged five. Mary became the guardian and entered on her bench which now embraced also Parks. One of her first acts was to obtain a licence to let the farm. She then got into serious trouble by felling and burning four oaks without leave. For this offence she forfeited the land on which it was committed and was readmitted only by the grace of the lord on paying a fine of £6, six times the value of the timber.

No further incidents occurred before her death in 1631, the same year as her son John came of age. His tenure of the property was short. Nevertheless, during it he married Alice Hayward, the heiress of Graunts on the Surrey border,[1] and in 1633 mortgaged the Sweetlands homestead and its land for £100 to Richard Yates for three years at 8 per cent. Not content with this he borrowed £40 more in December 1634. Soon afterwards he died leaving Alice his widow with an infant son Richard. The mortgage was a hindrance to Alice's bench. But Yates surrendered the security to her for her life with remainder to her husband's heirs. On this she had to pay a fine of £25. A marginal note in the Court Book explains the transaction as follows: 'This was in mortgage to Mr. Yates anno 1633 and the other in December 1634, now the mortgage was forfeited.'

When, therefore, Alice died in 1660, her son Richard was admitted. He had recently married Margaret, the widow of George Rapley of Stillands Farm on the Surrey border,[2] thus securing control over its 118 acres so long as his wife lived. But his short career as a mortgagor and his wife's death in 1668 deprived him of all, except Graunts, which, on his death, passed to his third cousin Richard of Knowles. He began his mortgaging in 1660

[1] Below, p. 87. [2] Below, p. 89.

by raising £150 on Sweetlands and Parks from William Ede who lived in Kirdford. The next year he enlarged the debt to £250 by transferring the mortgage to Thomas Stradling for seven years, and finally increased the sum to £310. In December 1668, six months after Margaret's death, Stradling foreclosed. That, however, was not the end. His son Thomas Stradling mortgaged the land for £300 with Humphrey Jewkes of Petworth, gent., an active mortgagee[1] who in September 1684 forced a sale to George Rapley, a London cordwainer of the Stillands Farm family. William Stent's Knowles, on the other hand, escaped this fate, and his great-great-grandson Richard was admitted to it and to Graunts free of encumbrance in 1707.

Walking northwards from widow Shertowe's cottage past John Shude's house and Colehook Mill one entered Colehook (now West) Wood, having on the right the Elkham[2] copyhold of 16 acres—3 arable, 10 pasture, and 3 meadow. The house had been built in 1565 by Robert ffyst who died before he could roof it. His widow was ordered to thatch it before Candlemas on pain of 20*s.* In 1610 an outhouse had been added and William Coxe was the copyholder. He remained in peaceful possession until he died in November 1637. His son Edward succeeded him on a fine of £14. Ten years later, as a first step, like Anthony Boyes, he mortgaged only 9 acres for £30 to his neighbour John Flower who was farming Steers and Combers on the other side of Colehook Wood with his house on the present site of Horton's Farm buildings. There followed a further advance of £10 from Flower: and the £40 was still due when Edward died and his brother John was admitted in 1654/5. John added £15 before his death in 1657/8. Only after a long interval did the next heir appear. No one, not even the mortgagee, responded to the three proclamations, and there is no record of John Coxe's admission except that he died in

[1] Below, pp. 134–5.

[2] Map VI.

possession in June 1662. He kept the mortgage alive and handed it on to his son Edward, who transferred it with an extra £15 to Richard Stent of Knowle. The total was now £70. It grew to £80 in 1667 with Henry Goble as mortgagee, the principal being repayable at his house in Petworth. In 1674 the Rev. Isaac Woodruff of Northchapel took it over, and adding £20 raised it after an existence of twenty years to a round £100. This was the last Coxe transaction before Edward and the Rev. Isaac sold the premises to Thomas North, the fine being assessed at £12. 10*s.* 0*d.* Still the property remained mortgaged, for North borrowed £60 towards the purchase money from the Rev. John Price, Rector of Petworth, the sum being repayable 'in the hall of the Parsonage', where the Rev. John acknowledged its receipt on 30 July 1690.

So far so good. But Thomas North proceeded to build up another debt by a mortgage to Mary Bromfield of Petworth, widow, for £5—a modest sum which two years later he expanded to £140 in a transfer to Lawrence Woodhatch. When he died in December 1694 Woodhatch was admitted. His fine was only £5. 15*s.* 0*d.*, but this was due to his simultaneous surrender of the premises to himself and his wife on which the lord received a second fine of a like amount. With the property thus in trust it was again mortgaged for £40 at 4 per cent., and this liability was not paid off until September 1726, ten years after Lawrence's death and while his widow was occupying it as her bench.

Thus during ninety years £340 was raised on these 16 acres by five mortgagors from nine mortgagees. There are now no buildings on the site nor other indication of how this large sum was spent, and Elkhams is now part of Pheasant Court Farm. So also are Robin Hood's Garden and widow Magicke's[1] Laces, which were

[1] Map VI.

on the opposite side of the common to the west. In 1610 John Orton lived in Robin Hood's habitation at 1*s.* a year. There is now a ruined cottage on the site. Laces was the tenement that widow Magicke tried to let without a licence. It was then of 30 acres—8 arable, 20 pasture, and 2 meadow. It yielded a rent of only 6*s.* When she died in 1612/13 her son surrendered it to the 9th Earl. As a demesne farm it was let at first to two tenants at 7*s.* 11*d.* an acre. In 1651 the whole was leased to John Burrell[1] at 8*s.* In addition he was required to repair the house and the barn which were said to be ruinous. He was allowed rough timber for this purpose at the beginning of his twenty-one year term. The boundaries here remain as they were in 1610.

On leaving Colehook Wood the visitor joined the way leading from Northchapel to the ironworks in Michel Park at the point where Peacock's farmhouse now is. In 1610 there was here only a cottage called Harrison's.[2] Walking towards Northchapel he passed John Flower's Steers and Combers and Robert Belchamber's Garlands and John Belchamber's Shonks.[3] Both these copyholds passed to other families by the marriages of two great-grand-daughters of Robert Belchamber, who died in 1571 (see table, p. 80). The one hitch in this record was when Elizabeth's father, after surrendering Garlands to himself for life with remainder to her, delayed for fourteen months paying the fine of £9. The court was obliged to order the seizure of the property if the money was not produced at the next court.[4]

Northchapel in 1610 had nine houses in it, and the chapel, numbered 6 to 15 in map IV. Number 6 at the corner of the common and the London Way was Thomas Osborne's rented at 1*s.* Number 7 was the chapel. Number 8 was occupied by Robert Wilton at the same

[1] Is he the origin of the name Burrell's Wood?

[2] Map II. [3] Map III. [4] See below, p. 88.

rent. Numbers 9 and 10 were the village residences of Thomas Andrews and John Magicke, who held substantial copyholds outside. In number 11 lived widow Dawborne paying a rent of 4*d*. Number 12 was Robert Goodier's. He died six years later leaving Agnes, his widow, and a son aged ten. A piglet was taken as a heriot and Agnes was admitted to her bench on a fine of

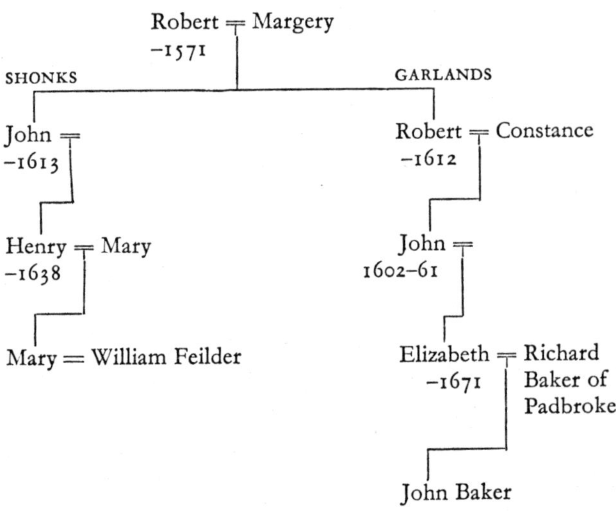

£1. 13*s*. 4*d*. Her rent was 1*s*. Number 13, rented at 1*s*., was the tenement for which Henry Pullen failed to pay the fine of £3. 10*s*. 0*d*. on the surrender of Christopher Flower. After the customary three proclamations he was still in default, though he gained admission ultimately. Number 14 was Walter Payne's, rent 6*d*. Dying in 1617, he left a widow, Elizabeth, and a son, Robert. Elizabeth occupied her bench for forty years. Robert then at last gained admission on a fine of £3. 10*s*. 0*d*. Number 15 was outside the manorial jurisdiction.[1]

Walking thus through Northchapel led the visitor towards Petworth past John Magicke's copyhold, now

[1] Map IV.

included in Goffe's Farm with its house dated 1654 and bearing the initials of William Yaldwin, to where the road to Lurgashall branched off westward along the northern boundary of Thomas Andrews's land.[1] The first point on this road was a gate marked on the 1610 map as 'This gate parteth Lurgashall and Northchapel'. It has now disappeared, but the boundary remains. The road then veered towards Navant Hill and Hill Grove. It did so until some date between 1795 and 1813 when it was diverted southward in a direct line to Lurgashall.[2] In 1610 it passed through the copyhold lands of Richard Wilshire covering 71 acres of which his mother Alice occupied only 35 and the house as her bench. She was a daughter of Margaret, widow of John Aylwyn, who had held as her bench 11 acres of Homdene. To this estate Alice had claimed in 1587 to be admitted as John Aylwyn's heir. But as she failed to exhibit the copy of court roll on which she relied, an inquiry into her pretensions was ordered. Opposed to her was another claimant, Stephen Ede, on what ground is not stated. With the consent of the manorial court he went to law in support of it and having won his case he was admitted on a fine of £10. Alice, therefore, had to be content with her Wilshire estate bench.

On Hillgrove Common was one cottage which successive John Tribes held for more than a century from 1581. The last of the line mortgaged it for £30. But he paid this off and his widow was admitted to her bench. There was no John Tribe to succeed her. The cottage had 1½ acres attached to it, and heriots levied on it were in 1669 a cow worth 50*s.* and in 1687 an ox valued at 20*s.* They had the run of the common.

Passing by Hillgrove the visitor continued northwards

[1] Map V.

[2] Gardner and Yeakell's map 1795 shows only the road to Navant Hill. The Ordnance Survey of 1813 shows also the direct road to Lurgashall.

by Bullocks Lane into Jobsons Lane and so to Gospel Green.[1] Here he paused for some time as it was a centre of manorial copyholds. To the north-west was Dickhurst or Doumans of 93 acres of which only 13 were arable. Moreover, its northern end was dominated by a 36-acre close of 'scrubbed bushes and birches', while at the opposite end were 13 acres covered with 'myne pittes'. Traces of them are still visible on the ground. Widow Alice Ede was then in occupation of the property as her bench, her house being on the same site as the present farm buildings. When she died in 1611 her son Henry was admitted. His uneventful but secure tenancy lasted until 1635. His widow Margaret then claimed her bench but died before she could be admitted. She had, however, already paid her fine of £20. When, therefore, her infant son Richard became the copyholder this sum plus £2 was taken as his fine. His uncle Richard Ede, of whom also he was fated to be the heir, was appointed his guardian.

This uncle was already a man of property, having been admitted in 1617 to the nearby copyhold, Redlands, after a delay in raising the fine of £40. This copyhold was a block of 97 acres with an outlying 18 acres near Gospel Green called Braches:

	Acres	
In the block		
House and orchard	1	
Arable land	54	
Pasture	20	
Meadow	1	
Wood	21	
	—	97
Braches		
Pasture with timber of 60 years' growth	14	
Meadow	4	
	—	18
		115

[1] Map I.

The large acreage of wood perhaps accounts for two pigs being the only heriot available in 1561, there being 'no better animal than a pig' on the property. In that year John Stonor had surrendered it to John Redman, husband of Stonor's sister Izoda. Redman then transferred it to John Pollard subject to Stonor having a lease of it during Izoda's life and after her death *un cubiculun* on it and a seven-acre croft. From John Pollard it passed to William Pollard, who left a widow but no heir when he died. The court therefore ordered an inquiry to discover who might claim the heritage. Meanwhile the regular proclamations were made. No one replied to the first two, not even the widow. At the third in December John Byrymble, the bailiff and collector, did so on her behalf, excusing her as being 'gravida' (with child). A further postponement followed until 9 January when the fact was established that she now had a daughter Joan aged 16 days. In due course Joan married William Christmas, to whom she brought Redlands and the 18 acres near Gospel Green as her dower.

William Christmas was a bad tenant, under whom the property passed to the Edes of Dickhurst. In 1605 Stephen and John Aylwyne, both of whom had served as messors, John Sturt, who had filled the office in 1599/1600, William Miles of Blackwool, John Magicke of Northchapel, and Robert Belchamber of Garlands were appointed to inspect the woods on his copyhold. On their report he was amerced for selling underwood without a licence. Twelve years later, in June 1617, he and Joan sold out to Richard Ede. From Richard the farm passed, after the death of his widow Margaret, to his nephew the youthful Richard Ede of Dickhurst.[1] Finally, to this Richard came also Little Braunchers[2] at Gospel Green on the death of his other uncle Thomas. When, therefore,

[1] *For note see foot of next page.*

[2] Map I.

he embarked on his short career as a mortgagor he had available as security:

	Acres
Dickhurst	93
Redlands	115
Little Braunchers . . .	11
	219

He first ventured with Little Braunchers in 1667. In 1610 it had been classified as one-third arable and two-thirds pasture. The £90 advanced for six years at 5 per cent. on its security alone seems a large sum. But John Rapley the mortgagee was satisfied with the bargain and was content to foreclose when Richard failed to repay him. Redlands was the next to be pledged, again in 1667. The sum raised this time was £350 from William Sadler the Chiddingfold blacksmith. Compared with the £8 per acre of Little Braunchers the £4. 6*s*. 9*d*. per acre of Redlands seems moderate. But again Richard was unable to meet the obligation and the farm passed into the possession of John Clements of Southampton. Finally, the 93 acres of Dickhurst were pledged to Richard Styles of River Park in Tillington for £250, or £2. 13*s*. 9*d*. an acre for six years at 6 per cent.; and Richard borrowed £20 more on it, an addition of 4*s*. 3*d*. an acre, by a transfer of the mortgage to one of the Fogdens of Fittleworth, who were active mortgagees. Thereafter Dickhurst followed Redlands

Note 1 from previous page.

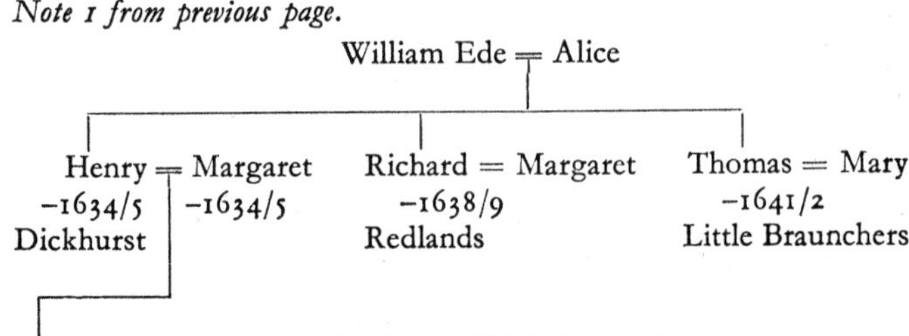

into the possession of Mr. Clements of Southampton. Thus in ten years Richard had raised the large sum of £710 on 219 acres and had lost them all.

Beyond Dickhurst to the west was Boxalls of 107 acres, of which 46 were arable. Its mortgage history resembled Dickhurst's except that the youthful mortgagor was rescued by his father-in-law.

In Henry VIII's reign George Cholwin was the copyholder and his widow Juliana occupied it as her bench until 1560. She was then succeeded by her son John, aged seven. His uncle Thomas was his nearest living relative, but was also the next heir. His appointment as guardian was therefore inappropriate and Augustine Pennicod was substituted. Pennicod at once applied for a licence to let the property for seven years and this was granted. Soon afterwards his status was undermined by John's death, for Thomas objected to being excluded from the property by the lease. He complained to the court, and a committee 'indifferently elected and chosen by the parties' and consisting of:

Thomas Smith, father of John Smith[1]
James Morley of Brockhurst and Bullreadings[2]
William Hamlin of Warres in Barewell[3]
Richard Etherton

was appointed to settle the dispute. They recommended a compromise, awarding Pennicod and his assigns a parcel of land of an annual value of 6*s*. 8*d*. for ten years rent free to be demarcated by another committee. To Thomas Cholwin they gave the remainder with the limitation that Pennicod should have the first option to rent it 'as another will' should Thomas decide to let it.

Thomas died in 1581 shortly before this agreement expired. His heir was his only daughter Joan. Born in

[1] Below, Chap. 5.
[2] Map I.
[3] Map XV.

1565 she was then 'fifteen and a little more', but nevertheless was wife of Thomas Steyning. The question then arose whether her husband or someone else should be her guardian. Her admission was twice postponed while diligent inquiries were made into 'what the custom of the manor was in such a case'. In the result her husband was not appointed and she became the ward of Richard Goble of Bishops until she was eighteen on condition that he allotted her 'what was reasonable'.

Another example of a husband not being guardian of his infant wife happened five years later. Charity Miles's father Richard had died in 1572 as copyholder of two fields; one of 6 acres, then called 'Sadlers', was described as 'lying within the Mill Gate'. This gate is not shown on the 1610 map but seems to have been in Mill Lane where the Haslingbourne Lane crossed it. The two fields were his mother's in her own right and had been surrendered to him by her when she remarried as a widow. When Richard died his widow Joan claimed her bench in them while Charity sought to be recognized as heir. But her grandmother declared that her surrender to Richard had been only for his life and that the reversion was hers. The court, after adjourning its decision, dismissed the grandmother's contention and admitted Joan as bencher and Charity as heir. When Charity inherited the property as an infant and married Richard Brookes, Richard Yates was her guardian. Was Brookes then to replace Yates? The answer was no.

One result of Joan Cholwin's marriage with Thomas Steyning was that the land became known as Steynings and it is so called in the 1610 terrier. It had then been surrendered to Richard Boxall, the progenitor of its Boxall name which survives to this day in Boxalland Farm and Boxalland Copse.

Richard, like Thomas Cholwin, left a sole heiress Joan, who married Thomas Albery. When, therefore, she died in 1640, her son Henry Albery succeeded as an infant of twelve, the fourth infant in succession. As soon as he reached his majority, having already married yet another Joan, daughter of William Coates, he began a career of mortgaging by borrowing £80 at 7 per cent. from his father, who had been his guardian. Three years later he transferred the liability to William Ayling of Stedham, increasing the amount to £100, or a little more than £1 an acre, at 6 per cent. for three years. Even this, however, proved too heavy a burden and he had to be rescued by his father-in-law who liquidated the mortgage and took over the property on a fine of £50 and a heriot of an ox worth £4. Having thus secured the estate Coates entailed it on himself and his wife with remainder to Henry and Joan and their heirs. Thus was it saved for their son William.

To the east of Dickhurst was Graunts or Grants, of triangular shape, 42 acres—15 arable, bounded on all sides by roads: the London Way on the east, the track to Gospel Green on the south, and the road (now closed) from Cripplecrouch Hill to the Green on the west. Margaret Upfold had it as her bench in 1610 but, with the assistance of her second husband, John Hayward, surrendered it to her son John. But being unable to pay the fine he surrendered to his stepbrother John Hayward, who paid the fine.[1] When in turn John died in 1633 his only child Alice succeeded him and carried Graunts to the Stents by marrying John of Sweetlands.

On leaving Gospel Green the visitor took the road towards Shillinglee and, after crossing the London Way, had on his left the Stilland, Padbroke, and Quennels copyholds. The former, of 98 acres, arable 12, was then held by John Rapley the grandfather of the mortgagee of Little Braunchers. His house was on the same site as the

[1] The account of this transaction is obscure. The above at any rate represents its result.

present Stilland farm buildings. In the 1610 terrier it is described as 'a tenement and orchard next by Broad Street by ye well there'. Padbroke and Quennels of 102 acres had Richard Baker as the tenant, his house being now the homestead of Potlane Farm. In the north-east corner of Padbroke was a close with 'quarry pittes'. Opposite Padbroke William Ede occupied a cottage, which is still there, and 17 acres called Fernhurst. Parkgate Farm buildings did not then exist, while the present Newhouse Farm, then named Beales, with 21 acres was occupied by John Flower of Steers and Combers. In 1779 Fernhurst had become Parkgate Farm of 18 acres, John Flower's 21 acres had been enlarged to 50 by the inclusion of an outlying copyhold between him and the Frith called Beales which belonged in 1610 to John Rapley of Stilland. The remainder of this area in 1610 was occupied by Mr. Anthony Finch's freehold called Eastland or Cradlers and by Thomas Christmas's Vering referred to in the next chapter. Finch's freehold was held by charter for a rent of 2*s.* or a sparrow hawk, a relief of 33*s.* 4*d.*, and a heriot of a mounter and harness worth £4. His widow Mary paid £4 for the mounter and 33*s.* 4*d.* for the relief.[1]

The Bakers avoided mortgaging and retained the two copyholds united until 1699 when they were divided between the two sons of Richard, the husband of Elizabeth Belchamber. The division may have been inspired by the consideration that at Elizabeth's death in 1671 her younger son John inherited Garlands by custom. His father therefore surrendered the reversion of Padbroke to the elder brother leaving Quennels to descend to the younger by custom. The fines paid and the heriots seized

[1] Finch owned also as copyholds a tenement and orchard in North Street, 4 acres in Limbo, Stanbridge, near Hampers Common and Upland (map I). Of Upland's 53 acres 9 were wood. Its rent as a copyhold was 13*s.* 6*d.* The 9th Earl bought it in 1620 and, retaining the wood in his own hands, let the remaining 44 acres at £12. 6*s.* 8*d.* or 5*s.* 7*d.* an acre.

on the successions of the three generations between 1617 and 1699 are of some interest. In 1617 the widow Alice took her bench for £12. When she died in 1631 Henry paid £33 on Padbroke and £17 on Quennels, two oxen being taken as heriots. In 1668 Henry surrendered his estate to his will, paying £20. When he died a month later his son Richard was assessed at £40 for Padbroke and £20 for Quennels, making £80 in all. His heriots were an ox worth £5 and a mare valued at £1, a compliment to the working ox. On the admittances of his sons, Richard to Padbroke and John to Quennels, the fines reverted to the 1631 level of £35 and £18. The heriots, on the other hand, indicated a change in farming practice. Only a sheep worth 5*s.* was available on each copyhold.

Rapley's Stilland was a consolidation of three copyholds: Stilland, Crabstock, and Fruens. They were united in Henry VIII's reign by Stephen Holloway, their combined rent being 33*s.* 4*d.* Each was subject to a heriot of an ox, and three young oxen were taken at a valuation of 26*s.* each when Stephen died in 1550. The Holloway family owned also the 14-acre freehold called Vering on the south side of Broad Street. After the death of Henry, Stephen's grandson, his widow sold this to Thomas Christmas, as is mentioned in the next chapter, for £50 or £3. 11*s.* 5*d.* an acre. How the three copyholds passed to the Rapleys is not recorded on any surviving roll. But here they founded a family as below beginning with John the copyholder in 1610 (see table, p. 90).

John Rapley, who was the mortgagee of Richard Ede's Little Braunchers in 1667, was the grandson of the John of 1610. He had come into Stilland in 1668 on the death of his mother Margaret, then the wife of Richard Stent of Sweetlands, as the younger of her two sons. On his death it passed to his daughter Margaret and so to the Butcher family. Nothing is known of George Rapley's migration to London nor of his establishment there as a cordwainer.

He must have prospered well enough to enable him to redeem Sweetlands and Parks from the Stradling mortgage of £300 held by Humphrey Jewkes. This purchase by him was completed only five months before his death, leaving a widow, Lucy. She entered Sweetlands and Parks as her bench, the heir being her younger son Henry. He, not desiring the inheritance, was admitted in August 1700 to the reversion in order to transfer it to his elder brother

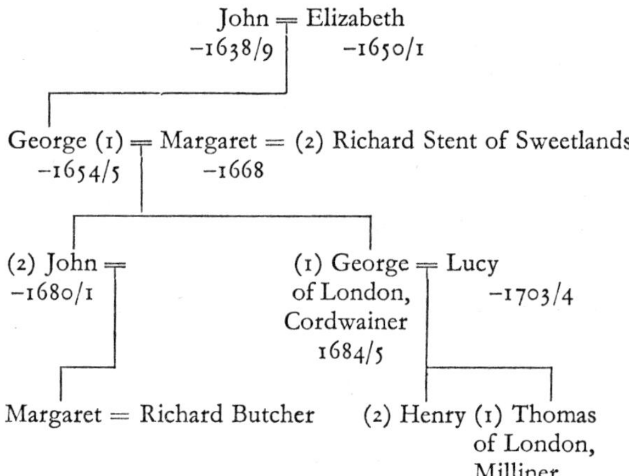

Thomas; two fines of £32. 10*s*. 0*d*. thus accrued to the lord. But Thomas had established himself in London as a milliner and had no wish to move to the weald. So he in turn surrendered the reversion to William Collens. No fine was levied on this third transfer. But when, on the death of Lucy a year later, William Collens was admitted as the copyholder, he had to pay £55, bringing the total for the three fines to £120 in three years.[1]

The visitor's tour of the manor has thus ended in the north-east corner. He has still to make an expedition to the south-west area. In other words we must revert to South Parkhurst mentioned in the last chapter. It was now demesne belonging to a group of copyholds in which

[1] His descendant in 1779 was the freeholder of Parks.

arable exceeded pasture, though not to the same extent as it did further south at Upperton.

Tenement[1]	*Copyholder*	*Acres*	*Arable*	*Pasture*	*Wood*
South Parkhurst	demesne	41	15½	25½	..
Sowters	Roger West	20	12	8	..
Westland	William Edsall	50	31	18	1
North Readings	William James	32	32	..	..
	Jeffery Hawkins	11	11	..	..
	John Sadler	10	10	..	..
		164	111½	51½	1

The reversion of Westlands was bought by the 9th Earl in 1613 when it was occupied by William Edsall's widow. As she lived until 1639 he never gained possession and the 10th Earl had to wait seven years. Before 1779 South Parkhurst and Sowters had also become demesne and had been joined to Westland to form the Parkhurst Farm. The survey of 1779 shows this to be free of woodland. The present Westland Copse was a later development. The three North Readings copyholds are now Nithurst Farm, Nithurst Copse, and Upper Copse. Nevertheless these changes have left the outer boundaries as they were in 1610.

The preponderance of arable land in these tenements was rivalled farther south in the land near the village of Upperton. Of 196 acres 141 were arable and the layout of the fields showed traces of the two-field system. Hence holdings were scattered, although consolidation was beginning in the seventeenth century. The history of the copyhold called Cradlers is to the point, and incidentally supplies an example of a deferred admittance after John Sadler's death in 1557. He had three sons, Thomas, Robert, and William, the youngest being the heir. But the widow declared herself to be with child who, if he were a son, would obviously be the youngest. Hence, as the court resolved:

The heir is yet uncertain for the mother doth suppose herself

[1] Map IX.

to be with child . . . and the custom is the youngest doth inherit.

In the meantime she could be admitted to her bench for an heir was available whatever happened to her. When she proved not to be with child the youngest brother William secured his right. After him Cradlers descended to his son John, while his brother Robert, whom we have noticed as a tenant of demesne land now in Frog Farm, owned also two nearby fields. When John died childless in 1626 the two copyhold estates were united in Robert's son Henry.

By 1779 consolidation had advanced much further and had also altered in character. Whereas in 1610 only about 13 acres out of 196 were freehold and all the rest copyhold, in 1779 the copyholds had sunk to 74 acres out of 185,[1] while the freeholds had advanced to 45. The third and the most important change was the entry of the demesne to the extent of 66 acres. Nevertheless, unlike Frog Farm, the demarcation of the fields remained in 1779 as it had been in 1610, and their occupation was still scattered. The absence of demesne caused the delay in consolidation. Meanwhile there had been considerable building in the village, which had assumed its present dimensions and plan.[2]

[1] The reduction in acreage from 196 to 185 was due to the making of the direct road from Tillington to Upperton in place of the previous way via Snowhill. See below, p. 117 and map XV.

[2] See the village as depicted in map XI.

5

IRONWORKS, OATS, MILLING AND MEDICINE

I. IRONWORKS

THE Petworth Manor had within its limits one forge and one furnace, the forge in the Great or Michel Park and the furnace on the northern border of the Frith.[1] Nearby in the county were at least five other furnaces and four forges. Local supplies of fuel, iron ore, and water power attracted the industry to the neighbourhood. Thomas Blackwell was the first operator of the Petworth Manor works as lessee of the 7th Earl of Northumberland. The lease has vanished. The date of its beginning is lost. It must have been before 1572. It appears to have ended in 1577/8, for in May 1578 the forge and furnace were let to John Smith, then only eighteen years old, and Sampson Coulstocke of Ifold.[2] In the indenture the works are stated to have been 'lately in the tenure and occupation of Thomas Blackwell gent'.

The Smith pedigree, so far as we need it, is simple enough:

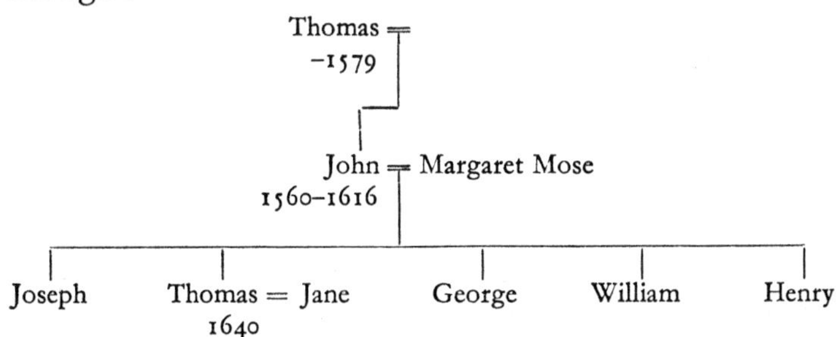

[1] Maps I and II.

[2] *Sussex Notes and Queries*, p. 240, note 32. Coulstocke leased Ifold from William Browne.

John Smith is described as the *generosus*, that is to say the well-born son of his father Thomas who had been rated more humbly as a yeoman. Thomas, however, had prospered. He had been a farmer of the demesne and a lessee of the kitchen garden dovecote of Petworth House. He was one of the committee appointed to settle the dispute between Thomas Cholwin and Augustine Pennicod over the lease of Boxalls. Towards the end of his life he entered the iron industry and was able to leave to his son the hammer at Wassell, to his widow part of the hammer at Dunsfold in Surrey, and to her and his son the lease of Shillinglee Park and ironworks. John inherited also his numerous freehold properties in Petworth. These included:

In North Street	*Rent* *s.*	*d.*
1. A messuage, barn, and garden near the fountain in North Street[1]	2	6
2. A garden and Dyehouse adjoining . .	6	0
3. A messuage against the Lord's gate (that is the Gate of the Manor)	3	8
Near the cemetery		
4. Pettifers, a name derived from a former owner. It is described as situated 'right against the church gate which leadeth from the church to the Market Place'. Later on it became the town house of Richard Stringer the elder[2]	8	0
Near the church stile		
5. A shop and a cellar		4
6. A little new-built house. (Both these became the property of the town)		6

[1] Living persons can remember a standard tap in North Street, but this probably connected with the supply installed in 1782.

[2] When John Smith died his son Thomas sold Pettifers for £174 to Richard Stringer. Appendant to it were a rood in Mill Mead and an acre in Budham Mead. The latter is number 34 on map XIVB. It is there entered as Dawtrey's, a previous owner.

In the market		
7. A messuage and a garden	1	0
In East Street		
8. A messuage and garden near the well and 4 acres at Keyfox.[1] (This house is marked in the 1610 map as John Smith's and we may assume that it was Thomas's also.[2] It was the most easterly house of the town somewhere opposite the present Angel Inn.)	5	6
Near Hampers Common		
9. 11 acres, part of Tanners Land.[3] (An ox worth 75*s.* was taken as a heriot.)	12	6
	40	0

Apart from the house in East Street and Tanners Land the town messuages were no doubt let at profitable rents. Some were already thus occupied when Thomas Smith acquired them. The reliefs due on them were one year's rent. Several points, however, arose over John's inheritance. He was still a minor aged nineteen when his father died, and so he had to wait two years before he came into his estate. He had already been admitted when eleven years old to the reversion of the tenement near the fountain in North Street, his father being his guardian on paying a relief of 2*s.* 6*d.* After his father's death another guardian was appointed. On John's coming of age and entering into full possession he was by mistake charged with only 29*s.* 3*d.* instead of 37*s.* 6*d.* for reliefs on the other eight items. This error was reported to the court held on 3 October 1581, and in addition a claim was made for a 2*s.* 6*d.* relief which was said to be due on

[1] Map VIII.

[2] Map XIIB.

[3] This part of Tanners Land is described in 1624, when it was demesne, as bounded on the west by the Kirdford road, on the east by the part of Tanners occupied by Nicholas Warner, on the north by the land of George Smith, and on the south by the Parson's glebe. Map VIII.

the appointment of the second guardian. In answer John contended that as some of the tenements had been let for terms of years before his father bought them, and his father had entailed others, the lord of the manor was entitled to only one-third of the full relief of 40*s*., that is to say 13*s*. 4*d*. He answered for this sum and no more. He was thereupon admitted. He then raised the question of his marriage and to whom a maritagium or fine might be due. He asked that a decision on the point might be postponed until the end of the Trinity law term to give him time to make sure that neither the Queen nor any other lord had a claim to it. He was engaged and wished to fix the date. The result of his inquiries is not recorded; but they did not interfere with his marriage to Margaret Mose, sister of John Mose.

During his life John accumulated a very large property. His Inquisition post mortem generously endows him with the manor of Ebernoe, 50 messuages, 6 tofts, 4 water-mills, 5 dovecotes, 50 gardens, 800 acres of arable, 100 of meadow, 50 of pasture, 400 of wood, and 1,000 of heath in Kirdford, Petworth, Tillington, Wisborough Green, and Fittleworth parishes. Here we are concerned only with the tenements listed above that he inherited from his father. To these he added three freeholds and three copyholds:

10. Sandham's House and garden in Mill Lane with 8 acres on Nightingale Lane,[1] afterwards absorbed into Frog Farm.
11. Two plots in Wide Mead.[2]
12. A meadow at Rotherbridge.

The three copyholds were:

13. About 3 acres in Fairfield[3] on the south side of the present Grove Street.

[1] Map XIIB, no. 40. This house is not marked in the 1610 map.
[2] Map XIVC, nos. 20 and 23. They are shown as permanently fenced.
[3] Map XIIB, no. II.

14. A barn and garden in North Street.
15. Three closes called Sones Crofts on the Kirdford road adjoining the Lymes demesne and covering 6¼ acres.[1]

On John's death in 1615/16 his third son George inherited these properties as the youngest surviving son subject to his mother's right to her bench in the copyholds. He was officially recognized as the next heir at the Court held on 13 February 1615/16, Henry being then reported to be dead. William must have died before him or he would have been the youngest survivor. Under George the estate was dispersed:

In North Street the messuages near the fountain and the Lord's Gate became the Lord's. The Dyehouse became the residence of Richard Aylwyn the brewer.

Near the cemetery, Pettifers became the house of Richard Stringer, for many years Reeve. The shop and the new-built house passed to the town.

In East Street the house and 4 acres at Keyfox were acquired for the Lord's demesne. The same fate befell Tanners Land also the meadow land in Wide Mead and at Rotherbridge and the 8 acres on Nightingale Lane.

Sandham's house was bought by Emery Puttock.

This survey of the Smith properties has diverted us from the ironworks. The close where the hammer stood in the Great Park is still commemorated by the hammer bridge on the road from Northchapel to Kirdford. With its Quarry Field and two Hammer Fields it became the central feature of the park in the sixteenth to seventeenth century. The way to it followed the route of the present Northchapel–Kirdford road passing through Belchamber's Garlands and so on to Ashlott's cottage, Pipers Lane, and Frithfold.[2] The straggling hammer pond covering 13 acres, with the 'tench pond' and the 'chapel pond', supplied sufficient water. A convenient rabbit warren

[1] Map VIII. This Sones is not the Sones now part of New Grove.
[2] Map II.

stretched from the hammer between the road and the pond to 'the close of pasture wherein the house standeth' on the same site as do now the Mitchellpark Farm buildings. The furnace stood on the furnace freehold, originally part of Finch's Eastlands and Cradlers freehold with a pond that overlapped his freehold and his Upland copyhold.[1] The 1610 map shows no house or other building on the site of the furnace. The lease of it to William Yaldwin in 1641 refers to 'the house, building and furnace' and 'all that messuage, house, buildings and tenement called the Founder's or Filler's house'.

The lease of these works to John Smith and Sampson Coulstocke in 1578 gives the following description of them:

1. One forge or hammer and all the houses and outhouses thereunto belonging, set, standing and being in the park commonly called the Great Park of Petworth.

2. One furnace . . . adjoining unto a certain piece of land of the Earl commonly called the Freethe.

3. All the cottages, buildings, hovels, sheds and lodges now occupied by the workmen of the furnace and forge or by the tenants of the ironworks.

4. All ponds, banks, sluices, floodgates, paths and ways usual for carts and carriages.

5. All waters and water courses, workmen's houses and garden plots.

6. All coal and mine places used or belonging to the works.

The lease then assures the following rights and liberties to the tenants:

1. Free access to and from the works with carts, workmen and all manner of carriages.

2. Liberty to take from the park in places most necessary for the works clay, earth, loam and sand, and the sand needed for the furnace.

[1] Map I. The drawing of the furnace is taken from the map. It is reproduced enlarged and not to scale.

3. Pasture for 12 oxen and 6 horses, and pannage for six swine.

4. The right to 36,000 cords of wood at the rate of 2,000 a year, the first four years free of all charge, within a three mile radius of either the furnace or the forge, but excluding Petworth Park. The lessees or their workmen being empowered to enter, after the feast of All Saints, lands and woods, as well freehold as copyhold, commons and waste to fell and carry away the yearly portion, the Earl undertaking not to sell wood within the radius to any others.

5. The right to take earth, sand, dust and cover for the coaling of the wood, and to make coal pits.

6. A supply of 20,000 great loads of mine at the rate of 800 loads and upwards every year at their choice, to be drawn by them. And the right to make the necessary mine pits.

7. Permission to take rough timber for repairs.

8. Authority to build a house for the Clerk of the Iron Works.

9. Timber for the pale posts and rails to enclose and repair the house, and to fence the garden plots of the workers.

The lease was for eighteen years at a rent of £100. No record remains of John's operations in the park as an iron master. His use of it for pasture was limited by his lease. Meanwhile Frithfold had been let in 1592 to Robert Strodwyke of Kirdford for twenty-one years at £17. But John succeeded him, for in a list of tenants in 1610 his occupation of it is noted as ending in 1611, and in 1612 it is entered as 'in hand'. Frithfold had no connexion with the iron industry.

An abortive attempt to establish a second furnace within the manor was made in 1586, perhaps under pressure of the Spanish menace. In that year Thomas Stanley[1] leased Vering from Thomas Christmas thus acquiring:

All that place where some time hath been an open pond to make a pond and to build a ffornasse commonly called an iron fornisse for casting, melting and makyng of sowe iron, and

[1] Steward of the Household. Knighted 1604.

ground sufficient as well for the laying of cole, iron myne, oare and sinder, as also to make and build the said fornasse and all manner of such other houses, places and demises as shall by the said Thomas Stanley seem meet and convenient.

But nothing came of this.

The lease of the Great Park to Sir Edward Francis in 1614 providing for its agricultural development included 'all that iron mill called the iron forge or hammer, and all buildings, dammes, floodgates thereto belonging'. But not the furnace. Thus separated from the forge the furnace was let in 1619 to Thomas Smith, George's elder brother, for twenty-one years at a peppercorn rent in consideration of a 'certain sum of money in hand', in other words a loan.[1]

The inactivity of the forge at this time and the lease of the furnace to Thomas Smith are confirmed by the sales of iron ore in 1616/17. Of 333 loads from the copyholds 105 were delivered direct to Smith's farm at Wassell; probably for use at the Ebernoe furnace which the Smiths worked.[2] Furthermore for the eight years 1617/18 to 1625/6 the whole manorial output of mine was taken by Mr. Middleton[3] and John Mose, the tenant of Guntersbridge and John Smith's brother-in-law. In their first year they mined the large quantity of 663 loads and for the whole period took 2,358, or an average of 295 a year.

In 1627 the business passed into new hands. In that year William Yaldwin of Blackdown, an ardent parliamentarian, became the sole buyer of the manor's iron ore until 1652 when he was succeeded by his son. He was not tenant of the ironworks before 1641. The furnace remained in the Smiths' hands under the agreement of 1619 which

[1] The only evidence for this fact is a marginal note in the return of rents for 1640/1 as follows: 'This was let by the Earl for 21 years to one Smith for a certain sum of money in hand at per annum one peppercorn and expired in 1640.'

[2] *S. N. & Q.* xiii. 235.

[3] Possibly the John Middleton who leased the Idehurst forge in 1614. Ibid., p. 238.

was to expire in 1640/1. The hammer had been included in the demise to Sir Edward Francis and remained inactive save for two temporary leases. Mrs. John Mose, the year before her husband died in 1636, paid £40 for its use for one year. She was then also tenant of the Quarry Field. Again in 1638/9 Henry Penfold paid £56 for the hammer for a year. He had bought 942 cords of wood for £329. 14*s.* o*d.* in 1635. But no light illumines these entries. In any case they were temporary incursions, for as soon as the lease of the furnace expired William Yaldwin took both furnace and hammer at the same £100 rent now sixty years old: £45 for the furnace and £55 for the forge. The lease of the furnace describes the premises as they were then in some detail:

1. The house, building and furnace for making iron called the Frith Furnace . . . with all the wheels, bellows, implements and other things belonging.

2. All that messuage, house, buildings and tenement called the Founder's or Filler's house.

3. All that piece of freehold whereon the furnace and house stand containing 5 acres 2 roods 20 perches.

4. All that stankpond, pool of water used for the furnace, sluices, floodgates etc.

5. The watercourse and stream used for the bringing water to the furnace stankpond.

All fish and fishing were reserved, the lord having the right to catch fish and store the pond with fish again. Also he retained the right to let water out of the pond at any time 'without hindering the blowing or working of the furnace', the cost of all consequent repairs to be his. In return Yaldwin was allowed:

1. To take enough timber for repairs within a radius of three miles.

2. To dig and take from the copyholds, lands and wastes of the Earl in Northchapel and Lurgashall 250 loads of mine, every load to contain 18 bushels at the heap, the one half by

heap the other by strike according to the custom of the country.[1]

3. To pay £28. 2*s.* 6*d.* for the 250 loads [i.e. 2*s.* 3*d.* a load] and 3*d.* a load to the copyholders where the ore is dug, and to fill in the pits.[2]

Yaldwin was forbidden:

1. To dig more than 30 ft. deep for his ore.
2. To drain the pond 'to the extent of its not containing 8 ft. of water in depth'.
3. To sublet.

The slackness of the business during the previous decade is shown by the returns of purchases of iron ore by Yaldwin:

1630/1	189 loads	1635/6	107 loads
1631/2	396 ,,	1636/7	95 ,,
1632/3	55 ,,	1637/8	172 ,,
1633/4	..	1638/9	172 ,,
1634/5	..	1639/40	80 ,,

Under Yaldwin's tenure of the furnace and the hammer and by the opportunity of the Civil War the sales of ore rose to 191 loads in 1641/2, 323 in 1642/3, 264 in 1643/4,[3]

[1] Measure by strike: struck or levelled as opposed to heaped. *O.E.D.*

[2] The cost of a load of mine delivered at the furnace was:

	s.	*d.*
Royalty to the lord	2	3
Royalty to the tenant		3
Cost of digging	8	0
Cost of carriage		2
	10	8

That is all the available information on the cost of production of 1 tun of bar iron.

4 loads of mine made 1 tun of sowe iron
1½ tuns of sowe iron made a tun of bar iron.
1 tun of bar iron was worth in Sussex in 1648 £18.
19 bushels of mine made a load or tun.

The 19 bushels to a load differs from the 18 mentioned in the 1641 lease.

[3] 1644/5 is missing.

874 in 1645/6 and 408 in 1646/7 at a reduced price of 2*s.* to the lord and 3*d.* to the copyholder. After this spurt no more purchases of ore by him are recorded. He took only timber. This accounts for a new agreement being made in 1650, this time for two years. Under it his rent for the furnace was increased to £50 while the rent of the forge was reduced to £30 and he was to be supplied with 600 cords of wood at 6*s.* taken from any woods assigned to him within a 4-mile radius. He was allowed also £40 'for new making the ground work about the furnace with stone to be paid when the work is sufficiently done and to cover it with tile at his charge for workmanship'. In 1651/2 132½ loads of mine were delivered to him at 2*s.* 6*d.* or £16. 11*s.* 3*d.* It came from Colehook Common. That was his last transaction.

In 1652 his son William began with a seven years' lease of the furnace at the rent of £50. He was assigned 600 cords of wood at 6*s.* 6*d.* within a radius of five miles:

> He to be charged for cutting and cording but to give notice to such persons as Hugh Potter and Henry Champion shall appoint before any be corded so that they may join in seeing it fairly done, and to be at liberty at any time to appoint cutters, corders and colliers to join with those employed by him.

The enlarged radius for taking wood from three, then to four, and finally to five, miles indicates at any rate a temporary fuel problem. This also accounts for the increase of 6*d.* in the price. Moreover, when William renewed the lease in 1658 for ten years at the same rent his allowance of wood was reduced to 500 cords and the price was raised to 6*s.* 8*d.*—two incentives to economy.

II. OATS

The practice of taking grain at fixed prices in payment of demesne rents was introduced while Sir Edward Francis was Supervisor. Leases were made in 1616/17 with eleven Petworth and five Sutton tenants arranging for an annual supply of 45 quarters of oats. After the 9th Earl's release from the Tower and the ending of Sir Edward's service the situation was reviewed and a 'true particular' was prepared in 1622 of demesne land on lease and in hand 'worth to be letten for 21 years or longer'. During the next three years seventeen new leases were negotiated, chiefly for the supply of oats.

					Qrts.
2	beginning	in	1623	for	48
11	,,	,,	1624	,,	184
4	,,	,,	1625	,,	129
					361

Thus with the old leases a total of 406 quarters was provided. Deliveries were quarterly in equal quantities for the larger amounts, half-yearly for the smaller, and annually for the smallest. An escape clause declared that:

> If at any time the Earl desires to receive the rent in money and not in oats that then giving half a years warning in writing under the hand of the Earl or his officers before the first payment is due the tenant shall pay 8*s*. for every quarter to be paid in one entire payment at Michaelmas next after the warning.

Eleven tenants agreed to deliver also 115 loads of straw. The following table shows that the deliveries in four years after 1622/3, omitting 1626/7 for which figures are missing, were:

	Total due	*Total delivered*
1623/4	277[1]	182
1624/5	406	284
1625/6	,,	379
1627/8	,,	368

1

Old leases . .	45
2 leases 1623 . .	48
11 leases 1624 .	184
	277

Four of the new indentures provided for the delivery of 62 quarters of barley to the brewery. Soon afterwards others referred to wheat. A list for 1631/2 shows the position in that year under the old and new instruments:

Sundrie provisions in kynde reserved upon divers leases and payable by sundrie tenants:[1]

Wheat	*Barley*	*Oats*	*Straw*	*Capons*
at 32*s.*	at 16*s.*	at 8*s.*	at 6*s.* 8*d.*	at 1*s.* 2*d.*
104	166	384	115	78

The wheat was supplied, to the extent of 92 quarters, by William Neale of Rutlington (now Ridlington) Farm 72 quarters and John Neale of Kelsham Farm 20 quarters. John delivered also 40 quarters of oats. Being south of the Rother both these farms were outside Petworth Manor. They had been acquired for the demesne—Rutlington in 1622 for £1,841, Kelsham among the properties bought from Sir Henry Goring in 1606. Richard Aylwyn the brewer was the appropriate producer of 15 quarters of barley from 19 acres of Tanners Land. His rent comprised also 3 quarters of oats and one capon. But the largest contributor of barley was William Eier the butcher, tenant of the two Quarry Fields on the south side of the Court Ditch and now within the park.[2] The largest suppliers of oats and straw were the five tenants of Hoes Farm.

Hoes Farm is illustrated in map XIII. In the second half of the sixteenth century the Sachers were its predominant tenants. In the lettings of 1596/7 William Sacher took fields, 1, 2, 4, 5, 6, 7, and 8, totalling 56 acres. Nicholas leased field 3 of 17 acres. Together, therefore, they farmed about one-half of the 140 acres of the then area of Hoes Farm and more than a third of the 264 acres of the modern Hoes. They retired when these leases terminated

[1] Here and later, the grain in quarters, the straw in loads.

[2] Map XIIB, fields E. (E covers two fields in the map.)

and the 140 acres were then farmed to Thomas Milles, Thomas Pellett, James Ford, and Robert Holmewood. Unfortunately only Thomas Milles's lease has survived, but the description of his area tells us the holdings of the others. The lease is dated 20 May 1623:

> Four closes of Land containing by estimation 47 acres 2 roods and 11 perches . . . abutting on the west upon the land of Thomas Pellett, on the east upon the land . . . now in occupation of James Ford, on the north on the land . . . now in occupation of James Ford and Robert Holmewood, and on the South on Wide Mead.

Milles's four closes were fields 8, 9, 10, and 11, making 47 acres. Pellett to the west occupied fields 12, 13, 14, and 15, or 27 acres. Ford had fields 1, 2, 3, and 4, covering 42 acres, and Holmewood was tenant of fields 5, 6, and 7, making 23 acres. Milles's rent was 40 quarters of 'sweet, dry, clean, wynoed and marchandable oates' at 8*s.* the quarter and 20 loads of 'sweet and dry straw either of wheat or rye at 6*s.* 8*d.* delivered at the Earl's stables. Translated into cash this meant £22. 13*s.* 4*d.* or about 9*s.* 8*d.* an acre. Oat straw was apparently not acceptable.

Deliveries of oats seldom equalled the stipulated quantities:

	Quarters due	*Quarters delivered*				
		1623/4	*1624/5*	*1625/6*	*1627/8*	*1631/2*
Thomas Milles	38	19½	40	30	27	38
Thomas Pellett	27	19	25	22½	25	27
James Ford	38	26½	29½	35½	25	38
Robert Holmewood	15	15	15	11	16	15
	118	80	109½	99	93	118

In the four years between 1623/4 and 1627/8 cited above, 1,214 quarters were taken by the stables.[1] Of this quantity

[1] Figures are not available for 1626/7. Taking 10 quarters of oats as the annual consumption of a horse one can form some idea of the 10th Earl's horse establishment and stud farm.

the four Hoes tenants were responsible for nearly a third. Only in 1631/2 did they deliver their full complement. Henry Holland of Osiers, however, was the most regular supplier. His lease was signed in May 1625 at a rent of 30 quarters of oats and £6 in cash—£18 in all or 4*s.* 6*d.* an acre. Next year £2 was knocked off the £6 'for houses by him built'. John Mose of Guntersbridge was charged with 60 quarters, much the largest assignment. But he found it difficult to fulfil.

That the system did not work satisfactorily is shown by the figures of the 1632/3 audit. The total of oats due from 28 tenants was 493 quarters 2 bushels, which at 8*s.* a quarter was £197. 6*s.* 0*d.* The final account closed as follows:

	Qtrs.	*Bushels*	£	*s.*	*d.*
Delivered to the stable	204	..	81	12	0
Paid in cash	174	4	69	16	0
Balance still due	114	6	45	18	0
	493	2	197	6	0

Accordingly an amendment was introduced into all the leases from 1633/4. This reversed the former condition that the tenants were to pay in kind unless given six months' notice to pay in cash:

> Those who have subscribed to their rents do hereby acknowledge and agree to pay money for their several provisions according to this rental until they be required to pay it in kind according to the covenant of their leases.

In fact the fixed values put on the grain bore no relation to contemporary soaring prices. Hence wheat was no longer demanded and the Rutlington and Kelsham Farms paid in cash. Oats, however, continued to be delivered for the stud and barley for the brewery. But the receipt of barley came to be confined to Richard Aylwyn's

Tanners Land. The demand for oats and straw was maintained:

	Oats	Straw
1635/6 . . .	392	64
1636/7 . . .	303	64
1637/8 . . .	302	64
1638/9 . . .	212	80

Of the 212 quarters 177 came from Hoes Farm, Guntersbridge, and Osiers: Hoes 87 quarters, Guntersbridge 60, and Osiers 30. The prominence of Hoes as a field for oats led to its being appropriated as a suitable site for the 10th Earl's stud farm. Accordingly in 1645 all its 173 acres were taken in hand 'for his breed'. The next year the part that had been occupied by Edward Peachey 'was disliked' for the purpose and in 1647 other portions were condemned, and these 67 acres were let to John Sadler at a rent of £35. 13*s*. 4*d*. or 10*s*. 7*d*. an acre, leaving 46 acres still in hand.

III. MILLS

The production of cereals was, of course, subject to the lord's monopoly of milling all grain save that consumed on a tenant's own premises. There were at times five corn mills, one malting mill, and one fulling mill in the manor: one malting and two corn mills at Coultershaw,[1] corn and fulling mills at Haslingbourne,[1] and two corn mills at Colehook.[2] In 1534 the malting mill and the two corn mills at Coultershaw were let for £10 to John Trewlofe and Thomas Libard, together with the water course and the fishing in the river between Rotherbridge and Shopham Bridge. From this beginning the Libards became hereditary millers.

The next lease, which bears the 7th Earl's signature and seal, is dated January 1564. The lessee was now Jane, Thomas's widow, with Edward King, a Petworth

[1] Map XIII. [2] Map VI.

clothier, as her partner. For £140 'in the name of a fine or an income aforehand', in other words a premium, and a rent of £10 they leased for twenty-one years:

> All that his corne mylles and malte mylle . . . commonly called Cowtershawe with the water ffyshinge and all manner of proffytts, commodities, advantages and appurtenances.

This was a truly comprehensive and encouraging demise, but it omitted the river fishing from Rotherbridge to Shopham Bridge.

Thirteen years later (1577) Thomas Libard, Jane's son, rented the two Colehook mills at £6 for twenty-one years. The water for them was taken from two dams on the stream flowing from Blackdown, as it does today, past Northchapel and Pheasantcourt Farm. Later it joined the stream that drove the Michel Park hammer and together they flowed to render the same service to Wassell Mill. The sites of both these dams are discernible on the Ordnance Survey. There was only one dam before 1370 when John Kitchener acquired the right to construct a second dam. Thereafter an 'old and a new pond' are referred to[1] as, for example, in Thomas Libard's lease. The description of the premises in the lease reads:

> All those his two water corne milnes standing upon the two ponds called the new Colehook pond and the old Colehook pond nere unto the sowth syde of Colehok woode and commonly knowen and called by the name of Colehooke Mylnes . . . and all buildings, waters and water courses, ffyshing, customes, tolles, multure, customes of tenants, proffyts and comodytes whatsoever, with the appurtenances unto the said water corne mylnes.

In 1592 Thomas, being no longer content with the limited opportunities available at Colehook, got his lease transferred to John Smith for a premium of £20 while he moved to the wider prospects of Coultershaw and

[1] Maps III and VI for the ponds.

Haslingbourne. For a premium of £10 and a rent of £40 he leased for twenty-one years the Coultershaw mills, and the fulling mill at Haslingbourne for £2. The price showed a considerable increase over the £140 premium and £10 rent of 1564. Nor did he secure the same comprehensive clause covering all manner of profits, commodities, advantages, and appurtenances.[1] On the other hand a cottage was included at 3*s.* a year.

A corn mill was working at Haslingbourne in 1315.[2] In 1370 Edward Maunser took it as well as a site for a fulling mill at a rent of 9*s.* for both, the lord undertaking to supply timber for the new mill when necessary. One hundred and seventy years later (in May 1542) the bailiff reported that on the parcel of waste 'where the fulling mill from ancient times was' no trace of it remained. The court thereupon proclaimed the fact and Robert Humphrey was admitted to the plot without a fine on agreeing to restore the mill and pay a rent of 6*s.* 8*d.* He carried out his contract and the mill was working in 1583 when Richard Humphrey of Moore became the tenant on condition that if he failed for thirty days to repair the mill after notice given by the bailiff the lease was to be cancelled. In Thomas Libard's lease the mill is described as:

> That fulling mill at Haslingborne and all buildings, waters, water courses, customs, profits and conditions whatsoever with the appurtenances.

All fish and fishing were reserved and Libard undertook:

> to look to the fish in the pond[3] that it be not at any time imbesuled or stolen away.

In addition to his milling Thomas became a demesne farm tenant leasing in 1596 'six mill fields and four

[1] The lease demised three water corn mills on the river Aron [*sic*]—i.e. two corn mills and the malting mill. The 1610 map calls the river the Aroam.

[2] Percy Chartulary 396n[2].

[3] The site of the pond is still obvious today.

Inholmes closes'.[1] The distinction between the six open and the four closed fields is noticeable. His area was 53½ acres, and the rent £28. 10*s.* 0*d.* is about 5*s.* 8*d.* an acre. He was still occupying this farm in 1610 but, when the term of twenty-one years ended, a new lease was made with John Libard for slightly different premises measuring a little over 50 acres at a rent of £30. 10*s.* 0*d.*, or about 12*s.* an acre, £28. 18*s.* 0*d.* in cash and £1. 12*s.* 0*d.* in 4 quarters of oats. The differences between the two leases are shown in the table below:

	Thomas 1596			John 1616/17 Margaret and Smart 1637		
		a. r. p.			*a. r. p.*	
Six mill fields	1. Bottom	4. –. 5		1.		
	2. Mill	6. –. –		2. Mill	6. –. –	
	3. Holemead	5. 3. 17		3. Holemead	5. 3. 17	
	4. New Close	3. 3. –		4. New Close	3. 3. 14	
	5. Mill	6. 1. 32		5. } Mill	11. –. –	
	6. East Mill	5. 2. 1		6. }		28. 1. 14
			31. 2. 15			
Four Inholme closes	7. Blaste	6. 1. 32.		7.		
	8. Bevis	6. 1. 32		8. Bevis	6. 1. 32	
	9. Hole	4. 1. 3		9. Hole	4. 1. 3	
	10. Garden	4. 3. –		10. Garden	4. 3. –	
			21. 3. 27			15. 1. 35
				11. Long Croft	4. –. 17	
				12. Newick	2. 1. 29	
						6. 2. 6
		53. 2. 2				50. 1. 15

Newick was a plot of demesne land on Hog Lane placed between the site of the present Cricketers' Lodge and the wall of the kitchen garden of Petworth House. Long Croft had been a part of Tobias Badmering's copyhold, mentioned in the next chapter,[2] which the lord acquired from his brother Thomas in 1631. It adjoined Newick on the north side. Only a very illegible copy of

[1] The six mill fields are 16, 17, 18, 19, 20, and 21, map XIII. The four Inholmes closes in map XIIB, nos. xi, xii, xiii, xiv.

[2] See below, p. 138) and map XIIB. Newick is field G, Longcroft field C.

John's lease has survived, but it is endorsed with the statement that his widow Margaret and Nicholas Smart, the butcher, who was tenant also of the Lymes, and to whom Richard Yates sold Furtherlees and Inholmes, had compounded for a new lease at 17*s.* an acre or £42. 15*s.* 10*d.* for the 50¼ acres. In addition to this soaring rent that of Coultershaw mills had risen to £50 plus £2 for a house. Margaret and her partner were therefore paying £94. 15*s.* 10*d.* a year.

The importance of Haslingbourne as a milling centre must also have increased as the rent for its mills and a house was £17 when Margaret Libard, widow of Thomas, continued the tenure of it, this time in partnership with James Ford, a neighbouring demesne tenant. And her successor in 1645, a fourth generation John Libard, paid the same rent.

Meanwhile the rent of Colehook Mill had remained stationary at £10. But there was now only one mill there and references to the need of its repair give an impression of slack business. In 1601 the repair of the water course was ordered to be done before the feast of the Nativity of St. John the Baptist under a penalty of 40*s.*; and fifty years later the building was reported to be ruinous. Thomas Boys, a copyholder of one of the cottages on Colehook Common who had died in 1649, had been the tenant since 1634. He was now replaced by Ralph Carter, miller of Lurgashall, at the same rent; but in consideration of his undertaking to repair the mill and millhouse he was allowed the first year's rent towards the cost, the lord providing:

> timber and stone to be laid down at the place this first year but to be wrought and drawn at his own charges and the necessary timber assigned him as shall be needed hereafter.

He was also required to be bound together with Richard Milles the millwright in the sum of £40 for the sufficient repairing of the mill and the performance of the lease.

'The ruinous condition' was, however, a true presage of the future: and the end was recorded in 1673 after Carter's lease had expired. The lord of the manor then granted the site to Robert Trew, the maltster, the premises being described as:

> That tenement at Colehook called the mill-house and the garden attached to it and also those three acres and a half or thereabouts of which one acre and a half belonged to the said tenement and with it was generally used and enjoyed, and the other two acres were lately covered with water and called the millpond.

Amercements for failing to grind at the lord's mills were commendably few. In 1587 William Edmonds, a tenant of three of the demesne fields on Haslingbourne Lane, was amerced 5*s*. for not carrying his corn either to Coultershaw or to Haslingbourne Mill, handy though both were to him. Two months later he was presented for possessing a quern mill 'contrary to manorial custom and to the prejudice of the Lord'. He was ordered to remove it under a second penalty of 5*s*. The same offending implement was found in 1617 in the hands of John Stapler, who served one year as supervisor of the market conduit. The same offence of owning 'moletrinas' contrary to manorial custom was committed in 1673 by William Ede of Churles in Tillington, and by Robert Meriweather of a copyhold near the Court Ditch. After Robert's death this was occupied as her bench by his widow Katherine. She was a Boxall and sister of Mary, the wife of Alexander Ross a London physician.[1] After her death the estate passed to the Rosses, the transfer being made possible by another Robert Meriweather, a wheelwright of Woodford in Essex, and Elizabeth Sturt of St. Bride's Parish in London (presumably also a Meriweather) quitclaiming all interest in it in consideration of £35. Subsequently it was acquired by the Duke of

[1] Below, p. 116.

Somerset and enclosed into his park. Robert Meriweather and William Ede were both fined 20*s.* if they failed to get rid of their offending implements.

For merely failing to grind at the lord's mill the fine was 4*d.* in 1628. In 1691 the penalty had risen to 12*d.* when three men and four women were presented for the offence. The court was indignant at this unusual contumacy and sentenced them to pay 12*d.* a month 'if it be not remedied'. Next year two of them, Jasper Peckwell senior and Elizabeth Holloway, were each amerced 12*s.* 'for not grinding at the lord's mill their corn for twelve months last past'. The other five had complied with the order.

Elizabeth Holloway was the daughter and sole heir of Nicholas Smart the butcher who acquired the Alderton properties: Furtherlees, Inholmes, and the Bakehouse near the cemetery. She inherited these and two others in her own right after the end of her mother's bench. She died in the Bakehouse a year after her amercement for not grinding at the lord's mill.

IV. MEDICINE

The earliest available record of a doctor is of the year 1586 when Christopher Johnson leased for twenty-one years the Fursey Crofts of 10 acres at the south-east corner where the Mill and Haslingbourne lanes cross. For some reason the lease was renewed two years later for twenty-one years at the same rent of £1, the land being described as 'at the mill gate on the east side of the highway from Petworth to Cowtershawe'.[1] Dr. Johnson was a distinguished Latin poet as well as a physician and his life is recorded in the *Dictionary of National Biography*. He was a Fellow of New College and Headmaster of Winchester for ten years until 1570. He then took his Doctorate of Medicine at Oxford and became a Fellow of the Royal College of Physicians. What he did with his 10 acres of

[1] Map XIII.

demesne arable land in the manor of Petworth is not disclosed nor is there any evidence of his practising in the neighbourhood.

The next doctor of whom we have any information was Dr. John P. Snagge. He called himself a medician and he was a purely local practitioner with no other distinctions or distractions. He lived in a house in the Market Place on the site more or less of the present Standen's tailors' shop, a site that is discussed in the next chapter. He died in 1672. One of his patients was the 10th Earl of Northumberland, and an account of his for attending on him has been preserved:

The Lord of Northumberland

1655

In p^r	a clyster	00. 02. 06
	a clyster	00. 02. 06
	a purge potion	00. 02. 06
	Cream of tartar	00. 00. 03
	a clyster	00. 02. 06
	a purging haughy ex cassia	00. 02. 06
	a clyster	00. 02. 06
	a purging potion	00. 03. 00
	Drachylora	00. 00. 06
	a clyster	00. 02. 06
	a clyster	00. 02. 06
	a purging potion	00. 02. 06
	a clyster	00. 02. 06
	a purging potion	00. 03. 00
	Burnt Alum	00. 00. 02
	a clyster	00. 02. 06
	a clyster	00. 02. 06
	Gruna sal tartary for poling	00. 01. 00
	Haughy ex cassia	00. 02. 00
	a clyster	00. 02. 06
	a vitrioll	00. 02. 06
		02. 04. 11

December 28 1655

Then Rec[d] of Mr. Lancelot Thornton the sum of forty-five shillings in full of the bill I say rec[d] £2. 5. 0.

Another London physician having a connexion with Petworth was Alexander Ross, whose wife, Mary Boxall, was sister of Katherine Meriweather. This generation of Petworth Boxalls was remarkably diffuse in their affiliations. Katherine alone of three sisters made an endogamous marriage within the Petworth community. Anne's husband was John Edsaw of Bury, Mary's Dr. Ross of London. Of the two brothers John emigrated to Haslemere and there set up as a mercer. Thomas, like his sister Katherine, married in the manor, his wife being Mary Quaife who inherited in her own right a tenement in East Street. Their daughter Anne, however, moved to Scotland as wife of David ffearn, a successful Edinburgh advocate. In 1694 he was serving as commissary or keeper of the consistorial (formerly episcopal) court of Ross, an office he still held when he died in 1731. He happened to be in London in 1694 on a matter concerning a bond when he and his Sussex relatives were involved in a complicated dispute over the sale to the Duke of Somerset of a tenement in Barewell held in a family trust created by father Boxall, and on the security for a mortgage which was somehow connected with this transaction.

The available correspondence on these subjects unfortunately contains no letter from ffearns, but only reports of his opinions. On the face of them these seem reasonable enough in so far as it is possible to understand the points at issue. But they aroused the antagonism of Mr. Thomas Brooker, one of the trustees, whose numerous letters are the main source of information. He gives the impression of an old busybody complaining of ill health and boasting of having served three Earls and one

Duke. He started life, it would seem, as a boy working in the garden under the 9th Earl. He continued in the service of the 10th and 11th Earls and finally rose to be auditor to the Percy heiress as Duchess of Somerset. On his evidence alone it would be unjust to criticize ffearns. Nor is it of any interest for us to do so. On the other hand, Brooker's letters give some interesting information on other points.

He was living in retirement in his house in Tillington. This was on a site that is now enclosed within the paddocks of Petworth Park. It stood on the road which then went in a direct line from Tillington church to Snowhill.[1] On its site a century later George, 3rd Earl of Egremont built one of the boxes for his brood mares. In one of his letters in February 1693/4 Brooker wrote:

> Here now is Mr. Shatter's wife who needs some spirit of sack doubled stilled and my wife has been so long out of order she is out of stock. Pray speak to Mr. Coles who was acquainted with Doctor Cassimer who knows where to have that which is right good. A pint may suit.

We know nothing of Dr. Cassimer. But if he could not supply the double distilled sack it could doubtless be obtained either from Joseph Morris, the Petworth apothecary, or from his colleague Robert Trew, the pharmacopolist, who lived in a house called Geerings in Sowter Street. So today is there in London a Pharmaceutical Society and a Society of Apothecaries. Morris, it seems, conducted his profession at the Dyehouse near Market Place.

We may here recall the remarkable mortgage history of this Dyehouse. In 1658 Thomas Levett, who was then its owner, mortgaged it and its garden and shambles for £100 which in due course he redeemed. Six years later he embarked afresh by modestly raising £20 for one year from John Stent. At the end of the year he transferred the

[1] Map XV.

debt to John Alcock increasing it to £60. Three years later he passed it on to Leonard Rooke, adding another £20. Next year Henry Styles took it over, making it a round £100. Finally, in 1670, Styles foreclosed and so compelled a sale to Richard Bridger who, in 1680, surrendered it to Joseph Morris. In the first mortgage of 1658 it is endowed with a shambles as well as a garden, but not in the others. John Drew, its former owner had been presented in 1656 for throwing dye water into the gutter in Market Place to the annoyance of passengers. His successors never committed this offence. The tenement seems therefore to have ceased to be a dyehouse as well as a shambles. It had become the residence of an apothecary with a garden.

6

SKETCH OF PETWORTH

IN this chapter we propose to make a casual tour through Petworth, passing such remarks as may seem appropriate on the places and persons with which and with whom we become acquainted. We will start, for no particular reason, from the free tenement called Clapham in West Street, opposite the kitchen garden of Petworth House. Early in the seventeenth century it was a property of Elizabeth Ayer, mother of William Ayer, the husband of Benedicta, daughter of Richard Stokes the seneschal. Later on we shall meet Benedicta at The Parlour in Market Place where we shall be able to get some luncheon. Adjoining Clapham on the west side was another tenement which Nicholas Lucas (on whom we have no information) sold to the 10th Earl in 1653. In the next year Richard Ayer, Benedicta's only son, who was the owner of Clapham, sold to the 10th Earl a strip, $39\frac{1}{2}$ ft. × 3 ft. 9 in., on which a skeeling or skilling[1] had been built, to be incorporated in the Lucas property. Nothing further occurred in connexion with it before Richard's death in 1673. Old Benedicta was then still alive, and not requiring Clapham she sold it to William Burchett the younger, a sawyer by profession, who used it as a security for his marriage settlement. And it proved a good investment, for in 1693 he and his wife sold it for £140 to the Duke of Somerset to be absorbed into the policies of the new Petworth House.

When Richard Ayer died in 1673 Clapham was occupied by John Crowther a carpenter, George Savell, whom

[1] A local term for a lean-to or penthouse.

history mentions only once when he was amerced 12*d.* for making a dunghill in the lord's waste, and Robert Young. This Robert is of interest to us because he invested £30 in a mortgage of the cottage, croft, and smithy in Tillington belonging to John Farnedon, a blacksmith. John had become possessed of it in 1681 for a fine of £3. 5*s.* 0*d.* on the surrender of James Buck of the Middle Temple who is described first as a gentleman and then as an esquire, a rise in the social scale. Indeed he had a distinguished career in the Temple, serving as sub-treasurer. The importance of this office and his own financial status are demonstrated by his having to provide security of £1,000 and two bonds of £250 each before he could be admitted to it. He held it for fifty-three years. When he expressed a wish to retire in 1702 the Benchers declined to part with him and were content to appoint an assistant to enable him to spend time in the country for his health. How he came to be the copyholder of a cottage and smithy in Tillington is a mystery. His admission is not recorded. When he sold them he agreed that £20 of the price should remain on mortgage and this was redeemed by Young's loan of £30 in January 1684/5. In April 1685 John Farnedon died and the cottage, croft, and smithy became his widow Susan's bench, a piglet being taken as a heriot and a fine of 30*s.* The heir was James Farnedon, who followed in his father's profession. In 1693 he obtained admission to the reversion on the same fine of £3. 5*s.* 0*d.* as his father had paid on an absolute surrender. Another indication of the increased value of the property is that after James was in full possession he was able to raise £50 on it in 1699 by a mortgage for four years to John Ayling of Tillington, yeoman, who later became prominent in manorial affairs as reeve and an affeeror. At the end of the term the mortgage was transferred to Robert Allen, the Petworth butcher. In 1705 he foreclosed and surrendered the smithy and cottage and croft to Samuel Robinson the locksmith, an appropriate occupant.

From this excursion to Tillington we may return to Benedicta's Parlour in Market Place. The copyhold on which it was built was part of the estate of Thomas Turges which in 1614 comprised three shops and a plot known later as the wellyard. Leading to this was an entrance called the Long Entry which is still preserved in the passage from Market Square through the door beside Standen's shop. There were also two other parcels. One was part of a neighbouring tenement to the west called Teelings and the other, probably to the north, was part of Testernes. Simon, Thomas's son, sold his reversionary interest in these premises to Richard Stokes, Benedicta's father who, as soon as he got possession, built the Parlour as an 'Eating House'. When he died in 1630 the results of his enterprise were displayed in the following description of them:

1. The Eating House caled The Parlour, a new kitchen adjoining, chambers and cellars and a small garden.
2. A tenement and shop called Teelings and another shop.
3. Two chambers above the Long Entry.
4. A barn, garden and plot part of another tenement called Testernes.
5. The wellyard.

Shortly before he died Richard Stokes surrendered the first two with a right of access to the wellyard to his daughter Benedicta, leaving the other three to descend to his son Henry by custom. Having made these dispositions he died before Benedicta could be admitted. But the custom of the manor accepted as valid a surrender made by one who died before it could be presented to the court. Nevertheless, Benedicta was admitted before her father's death was officially recorded. Her father's preference for her over his son Henry was justified, for she added an ale shop on the north side of the kitchen and the ale-conners had no cause to complain of the measure on which she sold her ale nor of its quality. The only presentment against her during her long life was the very common one of placing a 'house of office' next the street, where it became an offence to passers-by. Her husband William Ayer had been supervisor of the church conduit and prominent in the water supply negotiations of 1626. He died in office as a churchwarden. Moreover, he was a landlord independently of her, owning by charter a tenement called 'The Crown' and a garden and barn in East Street, as well as two copyhold selds or shops in Market Place. One of these shops had been released from heriot in the reign of Henry VIII and the heriot of the other had been fixed at 12*d.* in Queen Mary's time. A month before he died he divided them between his two daughters. Elizabeth was then an infant aged three and, dying soon afterwards, was succeeded by her brother Richard. Benedicta, her sister, survived to enjoy hers and to marry John Johnston.

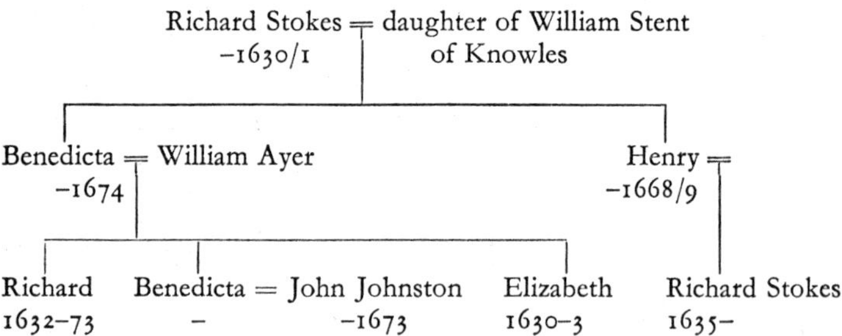

After her husband's death Benedicta continued to manage the Parlour. Her brother, Henry Stokes, possessed the two chambers above the Long Entry, the plot part of Testernes and the wellyard. These he surrendered to his son, Richard, reserving his own life-interest in them. Richard, however, had other ideas about his future and on coming of age released the premises back to his father and departing to Midhurst set up there as a cordwainer. Henry had taken the precaution of making the surrender to his son in the presence of Richard Stringer the elder in order to have a witness to the fact that he was not his son's guardian but had reserved a right to the profits for his own life. The court called on Stringer to testify to this truth. After the departure of his son, Henry mortgaged the property to his nephew Richard Ayer to whom it afterwards passed. In this transaction it is described as

> Three customary tenements viz: 1. a barn and garden called Testernes. 2. A tenement on the Market lately Turges's with a shop. 3. A piece of land called the wellyard and two cubicula above the Long Entry.

The shop that had come to Richard on the death of his sister was occupied by Edward Blysse, a butcher.

As Richard died a year before his mother he did not inherit the Parlour. In fact before his death Benedicta had entailed it on herself for life with remainder to him and then to the Johnstons. The description of it in this transaction gives us some information on the occupants. The new kitchen mentioned was now, of course, forty years old.

> A shop lately built with rooms and cellars in the market occupied by Thomas Willis mercer of Petworth and that other shop, rooms and cellars in the market lately occupied by John Snagge medician . . . and all the reversion and expectation on the death of Benedicta Ayer widow and Richard Ayer her son to the customary tenement called the Parlour, the new kitchen adjoining with rooms and cellars belonging, and a small garden with free access to water in the wellyard, and in the reversion and expectation in all that structure or ale house on the north side of the new kitchen, together with the plot and the two rooms over the long entry.

Johnston died in 1673 leaving a will appointing supervisors to sell all. After the customary proclamations they disposed of the shop lately built with rooms and cellars and Dr. Snagge's rooms and cellars to Thomas Willis the mercer; and in September 1677 he completed his acquisition of the Ayer properties by being admitted to the Parlour and to its appurtenances for a fine of £8. 10*s*. 0*d*.[1]

We may now skip a century and record that in 1836 Thomas Steer, late of Petworth but then of Midhurst, blacksmith, surrendered to George, 3rd Earl of Egremont:

> all that customary tenement being a parlour etc, kitchen adjoining and appurtenances and a little garden adjoining near the market with a free way or passage to the water in the piece of ground called the wellyard, and all that customary tenement with the brewhouse and other buildings adjoining to the north side of the kitchen . . . with a free way from the brewhouse to the water in the wellyard together with the blacksmith's shop and all other erections.

Again in 1842 'a little piece of ground called wellyard and a way leading from the King's highway to the north part of the said parcel of ground' are referred to. All remembrance of them has now perished.

On the west side of the Turges property was a copyhold of two gardens, a shop and other buildings owned by John Hall. Attached to it were 3 or 4 acres at the bottom of Shimmins Hill and a half-rood in Holemead. These had been surrendered to him in 1605 by Francis Teeling, William Teeling, a Petworth tailor, and Thomas Teeling, a Guildford blacksmith, quitclaiming all interest in them. At the very end of his life John Hall bought of William Goble the freehold on which New Grove House now stands and died before he could do fealty for it.[2] His son

[1] In 1707 the 'shop lately built with rooms and cellars' passed to Peter Luttman the butcher.

[2] In the transfer this free tenement is described as: 'a barn and garden and land appertaining thereto formerly six closes but now four of which three lie on the east side of the King's way from Petworth to Haslingbourne and the other close on the west side . . . on which close a superior house (speciosa domus mansionalis) lately built held by knight service paying at the feast of Easter yearly six capons or 18*d*. and reaping two days in the Autumn.' See map XVII.

John, however, carried through this formality. Having thus secured this desirable possession with the superior house that Goble had placed on it, he sold the Teeling property on which he had paid £35 for his admittance. The purchasers were Edward Martin and his wife Alice, the lady who made the unlicensed connexion with the water supply. The fine on this transfer was £50—a rise that may be attributed to a building referred to in 1632 as 'lately built', perhaps the beginnings of the 'Half Moon Inn', for Edward Martin served as an ale-conner. Alice's instructions to her executors to sell to 'persons willing to pay the best price' have already been quoted. Her executors claimed to have fulfilled them by selling to Thomas Moody for 'a competent sum', the lord of the manor securing a fine this time of £40. The 'Half Moon' now became definitely established with Thomas Coward as its taverner or vintner. This is proved by Thomas Moody's will bequeathing:

> All that tenement commonly called the Half Moon in Petworth with all that part that I now live in, with all the stables, barns, outhouses and all other appurtenances thereto belonging . . . all which were purchased from Anne [*sic*] Martin

to John Moody alias Graves son of Christopher Graves subject to an annuity of £5 to Christopher. He left also £60 for the fine on Moody's admission. There followed a riot of mortgages. Within a year John Moody had raised £250 from Samuel Snashall the mercer and two years later doubled the amount by a transfer to the Rev. Thomas Musgrave of Woolbeding. The inevitable result is briefly recorded in a marginal note in the Court Book: 'Sold to His Grace'. Thereafter this inn remained in the demesne of the lord of the manor until purchased by the Westminster Bank in this century.

Meanwhile the Grove had passed to the Peachey family, young John Hall's daughter and only child Mary having married William Peachey. The Grove did not become demesne until 1773 when George, 3rd Earl of Egremont, bought it with its 95 acres of farmland for £9,380.

Another shop described as being 'opposite the Market House' with room and cellar and a plot of waste 14 × 12 ft. was occupied by Henry Beech when he died in 1606. His son Henry, aged twelve, was his heir, but his admission was delayed while he was away at the 'Academia Oxonis'. When he returned to Petworth, having completed his studies, Sir Edward Francis, in the absence of any suitable relative, became his guardian. As soon as he was his own master he let the shop. Unfortunately this was his last recorded action. He died nine months later thus denying us the pleasure of following the subsequent career of this old Oxonian. As Rachel Grabwick then inherited the shop in her own right it seems probable that she was his sister. On her death in 1629 her son Humphrey was admitted as an infant, aged nine, with his father as guardian. On attaining his majority he sold the shop to Joshua Morris who was presented to the court five years later for encroaching on the waste and building a structure harmful to the people merchandizing in the market and obscuring their light. He would seem to have got off cheaply by being fined only 6*d*. for this accumulation of offences. When he died in 1655 his son Henry Morris sold the shop to William Hurst, an ale-conner. Its value is indicated through Hurst in 1662 raising £150 on it from Henry Luttman, who, however, was driven to foreclose.

The fact that Henry could invest £150 in a mortgage is evidence of his financial standing. There is no record of his profession. In 1659 he had been admitted to a copyhold tenement, barn, stable, garden, and backside near the Pound. In 1667 he pledged these for two years for £40 and so became a mortgagor. As the two years ended he died and was succeeded by his son Henry, aged thirteen. The mortgagee, however, was not in a hurry to foreclose and waited five years before he got Robert Scutt, whose business activities are referred to below, to replace him. Here a marginal note records that eventually the mortgage was redeemed and the house remained with the Luttman family for another twenty years.

Another Henry Morris and another Benedicta make us acquainted with Trump Alley and with a tenement and garden called Parkhurst situated somewhere to the south of Market Place on a site that cannot be clearly determined. Trump Alley was the only direct connexion between East Street and Market Place until it was supplanted by the making of New Street at the beginning of the nineteenth century. It still exists but is no longer used as a public passage.

The garden of Parkhurst abutted on the back premises of a tenement called the Bushe in Back (now High) Street occupied by Henry Goble. A path connected both, giving common access in each direction. This mutual convenience was confirmed when Henry Goble, at times supervisor of the market conduit and an ale-conner, in 1617 surrendered a new way to Henry Morris, then the occupier of Parkhurst, after 'the Lord of the Manor's officers' had annexed part of the old path to the neighbouring freehold tenement of Robert Trashe the inheritor of his cousin's violins. This action of the lord's officers, of which there is no other record, caused a war between the two holdings. Henry Goble died in 1626 and was succeeded by his son Henry, one of those who attended courts regularly, but got into trouble as an ale-conner. Henry Morris also was succeeded by his son William who surrendered Parkhurst to Joseph Clowser, an ale-conner. He appears to have considered that he now had exclusive control over the path, and proceeded to enclose his part of it into his garden. Henry Goble retaliated by heaping his part with dung and firewood.

The dispute came before the court on 15 September 1640 when each was ordered to restore liberty of passage to the other. The effectiveness of this command was demonstrated when Joseph Clowser's death was presented on 25 May 1648. Parkhurst was then described as a messuage, garden, and barn with egress and ingress under the gatehouse of the messuage called the Bushe.

A similar dispute, this time over a ditch, occurred between John Dee, who was so regular an attendant at courts, and Nicholas Mason, a tenant in Hog Lane. Unfortunately the report of the proceedings is incomplete, but it is worth quoting as particulars of such trials are rare:

> Whereas there is a difference between John Dee and Nicholas Mason about a ditch running at the east end of the garden of Nicholas Mason in Hog Lane in Petworth for the ending whereof they referred themselves to witnesses and Alexander Hardham and John Brookes being witnesses for the said John Dee did at this Court upon their oaths to the homage say as followeth viz: Alexander Hardham did testify that about twenty-five years since one Poore did say that the dike in question and grate did belong to Richard Hamon the owner of John Dee's house and that Hamon was to maintain the grate. John Brookes did testify that Richard Hamon about twenty years since did say that he did maintain the grate of that ditch and that the ditch was his: and that the said John Brookes had known the ditch for thirty years and that Richard Hamon took the doung (dung) out of that ditch.

The record ends here and the next page of the book is blank except for one small entry. The terrain of the dispute is difficult to locate. Richard Hamon is entered as a freeholder in 1615, but he is not given any freehold near Hog Lane in the map of 1610. Of the two witnesses, John Brookes has left no records and the available information on Alexander Hardham is not to his credit. In September 1605 and 1606 he was amerced for vagrant pigs and in the latter year for making a slaughter-house in his yard in the market. In June 1617 he was ordered to pay William Levett, the lessee of the Portreeveship and now owner of Peparams, 17*s.* 6*d.* by weekly instalments of 2*s.*; and finally in August he was found to be indebted to Robert Sadler for 39*s.* on a bond and for 13*s.* 4*d.* for which he had pledged a pair of curtains and a feather bed.

Joseph Clowser left Benedicta as his widow occupying Parkhurst. Thereafter she married two more husbands. The first was John Mitchell of Trump Alley. By him she had a son John, who succeeded to the alley and at the court held on 10 September 1672 was given the following assurances:

> We present that John Mitchell his heirs and assigns have free liberty of ingress, egress and regress at all times with carts and carriages through the passage or gates leading from the East Street in Petworth and adjoining the Little White Hart there... and hath been an ancient way time out of mind and is appurtenant and belonging to the said tenement of the said John Mitchell.

The exit to Market Place, which is clearly shown in the 1610 map, was described in another connexion as an 'atrium [i.e. a porch] to the Market'. In 1610 the alley had led in and out of an open square surrounded by the backs of houses. It is today cluttered up with walls and other buildings. Among the tenants mentioned as living in it were William Moore the collar-maker; Francis Catford and Henry Sandham, who had been registrars of leather, and Henry Morris the reeve in 1665/6. The 1610 map shows one of the houses on the East Street side as occupied by William Morris—he who was nominated as guardian of Richard Ford. A further interesting detail is that at the East Street entrance there was a barn occupied by John Ede, the tobacco-cutter, a skilling and a parcel of land used as a *caula porcilina* or pigfold, all included in John Mitchell's copyhold. In 1680 he surrendered the alley to his marriage with Anne Young. At the same court he transferred the barn and parcel of land to John Goble of the adjoining 'Little White Hart Inn', where Henry Rice was now the 'victualler'.

John Goble and his wife Katherine (a Barnard) remained in possession of the barn, the parcel, and the inn until 1696. Nathaniel Goble had by that time replaced John Ede as the tobacco-cutter in the barn. He must surely have had other financial resources than that profession, for in 1687 he had invested £70 in a mortgage of Wisdoms[1] then owned by John Aylward. When John died his estate passed under his will to Katherine. She at once got rid of the inn to Moses Roles, the fine on this transaction being remitted by the lord and lady of the manor.[2] Moses seems hardly to have deserved this favour, for in the next year, when he was appointed ale-conner, he was amerced 5*s.* for neglecting his duty. He followed the fashion by borrowing £50 on his new acquisition and by increasing the burden to £60 by transfer to another mortgagee.

The story of the 'White Hart' in High Street is obscure. We have already mentioned Henry Goble's bequest in 1670 of his 'new-built stable' in the White Hart Lane to his elder son in preference to the younger son, who was heir by custom. The description of the property in the will reads:

> My copyhold stable in the White Hart Lane being lately new-built by me together with a copyhold garden and plot in the said lane.

In 1711 Thomas Platt surrendered to his will a customary tenement and premises occupied by him 'being near the stable of the "White Hart" in Petworth'. In 1823 the 'White Hart' was one of the five inns of the town, George Knight being the innkeeper. Thirty years later it was 'a private

[1] Map VI.

[2] Duke and Duchess of Somerset.

tenement on the yearly rent of 1*s.* whereof Clement Robert Burgess, an architect and surveyor, and also a stone mason, died seized on June 18 1855'. It was then in the dual occupation of James Lane, a baker, who enjoyed a parlour with a bay window, and by a tailor's shop with another bay window. This description tallies with the appearance of the existing building with its two bay windows. White Hart Lane also is still with us.

On entering East Street from Trump Alley the principal feature to the left on the opposite side of the street was an open space called Lane's Garden, but after whom is a mystery. The open space is still there, though it is now hidden behind a high wall which was described in 1655 as 'the new stone wall here lately built', a phrase that may refer to any year within the first half of the century. Why this formidable obstacle was erected and by whom are other guesses. The history of the garden is also difficult to elucidate in the absence of a plan. The 1610 map ignores it altogether and fills East Street with a few conventional houses and gardens bearing no relation to the facts. The garden was divided into a number of separate ownerships, as it were allotments, ranging from 8 perches to 1½ acres. One portion was owned by Richard Stringer, the mercer and reeve, and on his death in 1660 his son Richard was admitted by custom. It is not mentioned in his father's will.

This Richard Stringer the younger was already a man of considerable wealth, as is demonstrated by the following circumstances. His father had obtained a judgement in the court of King's Bench for £1,000 against William Mose the younger, of Kirdford. As a means of paying this large sum Mose mortgaged in 1642 to young Richard the reversion of a tenement in East Street with a garden 'now walled containing half an acre adjoining the said tenement to the north'. This description tallies with the present situation of Stringer's Hall. The amount of the mortgage was £700 and included in the security were two other properties. The condition was that Mose should repay the £700 one year after his father's death. But he died before his father. Finally the father in 1651 quitclaimed all interest in the premises to the younger Stringer and so repaid the loan. It is suggested that this is the site on which Stringer's Hall was built. The date 1654 and the initials R.S. on the top of a rain-water pipe would seem to confirm this surmise. Moreover, in 1662 young Richard acquired two other East Street properties, one of which was upwards of 2 acres in size.

Against the surmise is the fact that the younger Richard's will refers to only two 'great houses' that were his. One, in which he lived, was in Back Street. The other was Pettifers, which he had inherited from his father. He seems to have rebuilt and enlarged Pettifers, for he describes it in his will as 'my great house built and re-building on the outside with hewed stone in Church Style Street'.[1] There is now no trace of this house. It must have been removed when the many alterations were made round Petworth House, including the creation of Park Road. Nor does the will mention any great house in East Street. But he demised all his copyholds in a general bequest to his niece Susan, daughter of his sister, the wife of John Cook, without giving any particulars of them. He nominated Susan as his heir in preference to her two brothers, the younger of whom was the customary heir. But Susan died before she could be admitted. Her father therefore came to the September Court in 1679 and claimed that her younger brother Richard, aged six, should replace her. He was admitted and his father became his guardian. The two descriptive entries of the East Street copyholds in this admittance are: A tenement, garden, and yard, and 2 acres and 1 rood parcell of a cottage. Together these may surely indicate the premises of Stringer's Hall.

[1] i.e. West Street.

Six years later the infant Richard died and was succeeded by his elder brother John. For some reason his admission was delayed contrary to custom until he came of age in 1689/90. In the meantime his father and not the lord of the manor, as the 9th Earl had endeavoured to establish, received the profits of his estate and lived in the house. Soon afterwards he deemed it necessary to make his will. Now at last the Hall is described as the 'capital messuage wherein his father then dwelt'. He left it to his parents for their lives, with remainder to Humphrey Jewkes, whose wife Sarah was one of the Stringer co-heirs.[1]

Like many other wealthy men Richard Stringer was moved to endow a school. He had inherited Bridgefoot Farm in Stedham from his father. This he demised to six trustees to found a free school in Petworth. It was to be staffed by a master and an usher, and to be for twenty poor boys or youths whose parents were resident in the town or parish of Petworth. Their education was to be in 'good literature and writing and casting of accounts'. The trustee governors of the school were authorized: (1) To appoint the master and usher provided, however, that 'no parson, curate, minister or chaplain whatsoever shall be Master or Usher at any time'. Thus the school was to be segregated from contemporary ecclesiastical controversies. (2) To nominate the twenty boys. (3) To make rules and orders for the good government of the school. (4) To receive so much of the rents and profits of the farm as they thought fit. (5) To let the farm by lease for terms not exceeding twenty-one years. (6) Once a year to inspect the school to see that the boys were being carefully instructed and to watch their improvement. (7) To admonish them to be diligent in their learning and the master and usher in their teaching. Finally, as regular meetings and consultations of the governors were

[1] This is recorded on the Jewkes memorial in Petworth Church. Quoted in Dalloway, i. 339. The inscription is illegible in the church.

essential, they were authorized to spend out of the rent 21*s.* yearly at such times as they met.

The six trustees were:

John Cooke, Richard's brother-in-law.
Henry Barnard, his cousin, a prominent citizen, who is mentioned below.
Francis Mose, the grandson of John, the lessee of Guntersbridge.
John Peachey, of the Grove.
Thomas Stradling the mortgagee of Richard Stent's Sweetlands and Marks.
William Moore, the collar-maker of Trump Alley.

There is no evidence that the trustees established the free school. Indeed the bequest strikes one as deficient, in that it failed to make any provision for a school house. But the intention was admirable.

We have already met Humphrey Jewkes as a mortgagee of Sweetlands and Parks. He made a much larger investment of £1,500 on the security of John Hardham's Manor of Dean or Dean Farm and £160 on three copyholds held of the Manor of Petworth, one in Nightingale Lane and the other two in Tillington and Upperton. Dean House still remains as a memorial of the manor. In 1651 it was described as:

> All that mansion and dwelling house, four barns and garden and orchard called Deane and two little closes of land one adjoining to the garden and the other to the toll gate containing half an acre.

Added to these were thirty-two closes ranging in size from 1½ to 8 acres and totalling 172. In 1667 William Hardham, John's successor, mortgaged these for £800 to Sir Orlando Gee.[1] In 1669 the principal, plus £100 for

[1] Orlando Gee (1619–1705) was knighted in 1682. He was registrar of the court of admiralty and was prominent in the Duke of Somerset's affairs, as was also his son John Gee, who was seneschal of the manor, 1673–83.

interest, was still outstanding. Nevertheless, Gee advanced a further £300, bringing the total to £1,200. With this he appears to have been satisfied, for in 1670 the mortgage was transferred to Humphrey Jewkes for £1,593. Not until twenty-six years later did Jewkes foreclose. This was a long-dated investment. The others were short-dated:

		£
Dean Manor	1670–98	1,593
Sweetlands and Parks	1683–84	300
Copyhold in Nightingale Lane . . .	1683–84	30
Copyholds in Tillington and Upperton .	1689–90	130
		£2,053

Thus in 1683–4 he had £1,923 out on mortgage. In 1689–90 £1,723, and from 1690 to 1698 £1,593.[1]

The Barnards, who were distinguished in manorial and other affairs, had interests in Lane's Garden. Thomas was admitted on the surrender of his father in 1626 to half a rood of the garden. Soon afterwards he collected another parcel 58 × 28 ft. from John Hall. In 1648 he surrendered both to Henry Barnard, whose relationship to him is not clear. Henry in turn acquired a tenement with its house 'new builded' in 1610 and owned by Agatha Prickloe in her own right, not occupied by her as her bench, as was incorrectly stated in the Court Book until officially corrected. When he was admitted he produced two copies of court rolls dated Hock Tuesday 20 and 23 Henry VIII,[2] proving that the fine due upon a death had been settled by custom to be the same as the rent of 16*d.*, and with this the lord had to be content. On this plot Henry built a stable. His son Henry succeeded him in 1673/4. These three Barnards were prominent in the manor. Thomas served five years as seneschal. The first Henry was an

[1] Only Jewkes's copyhold mortgages are included in the list on p. 12. Peter Jewkes sold the manor of Dean to George, 3rd Earl of Egremont in 1785.

[2] These rolls are missing.

ale-conner for two years, reeve for six, and an affeeror for two. The second Henry was seneschal for 1683–5,[1] and again from 1689 until 1693. It was his house that was used so frequently as a place for paying off mortgages.[2]

Other copyhold tenements in East Street had the following descriptions:

Tenements and gardens	7
Tenement, garden, and barn	1
Tenement and a plot 63 × 20 ft.	1
Shop and plot 27 × 15 ft.	1
A barn, garden, and a croft of 1½ acres . .	1
A hog pen	1
	12

The barn, garden, and croft were the scene of Nicholas James's attempt to evade paying his fine on admission with the result that they passed to Anne Page as mortgagee. She married Richard Robinson and had by him a son, Page Robinson, to whom the estate descended on her death in 1659. During his minority it seems to have depreciated much in value, for when he came of age and surrendered it in 1681 to Robert Scutt, the mercer and draper, no animal was available for a heriot (a cow worth 40*s.* had been seized in 1650) and the fine was assessed at only £6. With Robert the property recovered, as was natural in the hands of so active a man. Apart from his dual trade he served as reeve for six years, 1697–1703, and also several times as an affeeror and an ale-conner. His investments in land were mortgages. And with them he was prudent, his average in five such enterprises being £21. His son John dealt in larger sums. While his father was still alive his three secured loans totalled £120. And yet when he succeeded in 1706 to his father's two barns,

[1] He was appointed first as deputy to John Gee, who died in 1685.

[2] The Barnard family is difficult to disentangle as the parish register and the manorial records do not agree.

garden, and croft in East Street the fine he had to pay was only £11, compared with the £15 charged to Nicholas James more than fifty years before.

At the south-west corner of the street now named Angel Street, but in 1610 included in East Street, was Ralph Bowyer's tenement, called Kitts. This was the home of Peter Bowyer who gave evidence in the 1677 inquiry into the right of way over the glebe to Idehurst. He frequently served as a searcher and sealer of leather and as registrar, but had twice to be presented for failing to report to the steward. Under him the house is said to be 'newly built' with a shop, a garden, and a plot 27×15 ft. He mortgaged the shop and the plot to Leonard Rooke, the mortgagee of Cradlers, Blackwool, Redhill, and Warres.[1] In the result the shop and plot passed to John Lickfold, the blacksmith. Lickfold was already established nearby at the corner of the modern Middle and Grove Streets. His shop is still there although now seldom operating. When he died in 1702 his son Edward succeeded him. Edward was a too-active developer. His extensive building operations caused him to be presented to the court on 13 September 1709 for erecting a shop higher than formerly, breaking down a neighbour's wall, and interfering with his Ancient Light.

Next to Bowyer's house, on the east side, was John Smith's Petworth residence with its pasture croft of 1¼ acres.

Walking down Back Street, now called High Street, one passed on the left Pippets, the tenement to which Richard Ford was admitted in 1612 on the death of his mother, and on the right Henry Goble's Bushe; also Stringer's great house, if it existed in 1610. Pippets is described as

[1] Warres was in Barewell. In 1558 its area is stated as 26 acres. Thereafter it was split into several tenements of which Robert Warner mortgaged one of 4 acres to Leonard Rooke. Six years later he disposed of it, no doubt to repay the mortgage.

'lying between East Street and Sowter Street'. This is correct for the croft attached to it at the back is as shown in map XIIB, field 1.

After crossing Market Place one entered Sowter Street, now Pound Street. At the corner where the road to Tillington branches off was a tenement called Uphouse. Tobias Badmering was its copyholder, having been preceded by his father and grandfather. He owned as well another town residence in North Street called Skares and three separate crofts outside, among them Longcroft. There was some difficulty over them because his copy of court roll could not be found. On the other hand the admission of Tobias's father in 1559 had been accepted without question and can be checked today. At any rate Tobias died in possession and was succeeded by his brother.

Two houses were built in this vicinity by William Bamfield, by trade a free mason, before he died in 1650. Both were 'at the bottom of Hog Lane near the Pound' on demesne land rented at 40*s*. One had a tiled roof and the other a roof of thatch. Crescet Gibbs, the 10th Earl's stud groom, lived under the tiles and Bamfield under the thatch. On his death both needed much repair and new direct leases were made with Crescet Gibbs and John Washington, who was a joiner. Gibbs was to pay a rent of £3. 6*s*. 8*d*. for a twenty-one years' tenure, but as the house

> will require to be new stript the new tiling is to be forthwith done to his hands and towards the other repairs he is to be allowed a years rent free towards his charges and fitting the said house, the backside to be divided and fenced betwixt him and the other house.

A note, however, adds that:

> His Lordship having been at much greater charge in repairing than was intended, Gibbs is to have his lease but for eleven years.

John Washington also was allowed a year's rent towards his repairs, and he was particularly bound to preserve the partition between the gardens. A similar note records the excessive expenditure of the Earl:

> His Lordship having been at the charge of building a stone wall at the gable end which cost above £4 and allowing him now in money 43*s.* towards other repairs by him done and 20*s.* which should have been paid for next Michaelmas rent towards the thatching, all which he himself should have done, it is now agreed that his lease shall be for eleven years from Michaelmas 1651.

These two houses have disappeared; and so we can but return to Sowter Street. Next but one to Badmering to the north was the house of Peter Young. This was a tenement and garden carrying with it 'a parcel of land called Sones at Tinkers Croft by Nightingale Lane' (no. 32 on map XIIB). He was copyholder also of two closes in Barewell, and of the Sones which is now part of the New Grove garden. He occupied thirdly a tenement, garden, and orchard in Tillington, a rood in Holemead and in Wide Mead[1]—a typically scattered copyhold estate. But his chief interest was a freehold outside the manor. Next but one to Young was a plot of demesne on the site of which stands the present gate leading into the works' yard of Petworth House. In 1610 this yard was part of Culver Croft,[2] a name that still survives in the house now used as a school since the former school was destroyed by a bomb.

The tour has omitted North Street; so we must enter from that direction the town as it was in 1610. On the right hand was a continuous row of houses and small enclosures stretching from near the present, but then non-existing, Hamper's Common Lodge[3] to the back

[1] The 1610 map does not include him as an owner in Wide Mead.

[2] Map XIIB, field H.

[3] Map XV. The houses on the west side of the street are numbered 1–13.

entrance to the Mansion House. The first was the tenement and garden 'near the pale of the Conygre Park' to which Jane Howden was admitted despite her inability to pay the fine. After her death it became Aaron Smith's. Next to him was Gilliane Arcolde in a 'cottage builded on the common of Petworth by London Waie in North Street', again with 3 roods and a rent of 12*d.* The sites of these are still visibly marked although the cottages have disappeared. We know not who inhabited the third cottage. Anthony Finch owned the fourth at a rent of 6*d.* with a garden and an orchard. Its neighbour to the south was the property of Samuel and Dionisius Britton. Dionisius passed it on to William Kenton, an infant of whom he became the guardian. As soon as Kenton came of age he surrendered it to Edward Peachey, the haberdasher. John Morris paid a rent of 16*d.* for the next one of 20 perches and a garden. Next came Tobias Badmering's—'a tenement with a garden in ye North Street called Skares' of 23 perches. A freehold plot intervened between him and the copyhold tenement of William Goble, called Downams, which he soon afterwards surrendered to Aaron Smith. Beyond Goble were three houses whose owners' names are illegible on the map. And beyond them was the copyhold of Robert Hatcher, an ale-conner, and a plot of demesne land described as 'one house and parcel of ground lying behind the Pheasant Yard of Petworth Place next Hatcher.' The demesne plot was flanked by a freehold owned by John Smith. The 9th Earl bought this in 1620.

The change wrought on the west side of the street by the Duke of Somerset is shown on the plan. Hurst's house had replaced the Downams of William Goble and Aaron Smith. The Duke acquired it by an exchange. His operations, however, spread over his seventy years as lord of the manor, call for separate treatment.

The 1610 map records the names of no householders

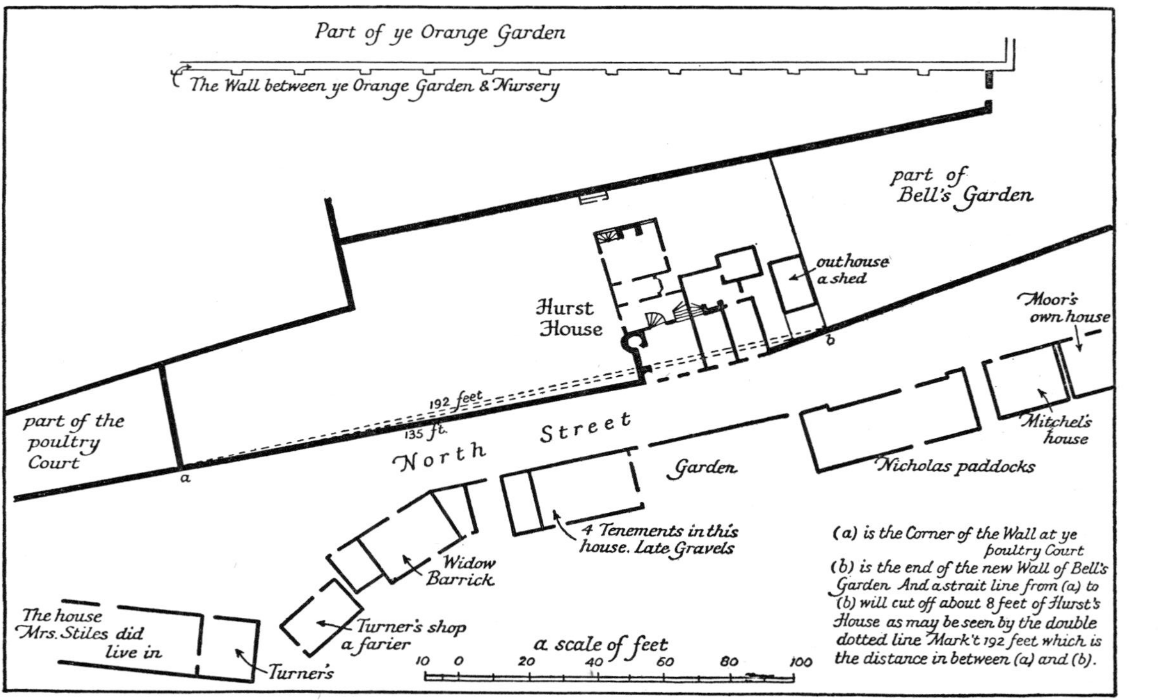
Part of ye Orange Garden
The Wall between ye Orange Garden & Nursery
part of Bell's Garden
outhouse a shed
Hurst House
Moor's own house
Mitchel's house
part of the poultry Court
192 feet
135 ft.
North Street
Garden
Nicholas paddocks
a
b
4 Tenements in this house. Late Gravels
Widow Barrick
The house Mrs. Stiles did live in
Turner's shop a farier
Turner's
a scale of feet
10 0 20 40 60 80 100
(a) is the Corner of the Wall at ye poultry Court
(b) is the end of the new Wall of Bell's Garden And a strait line from (a) to (b) will cut off about 8 feet of Hurst's House as may be seen by the double dotted line Mark't 192 feet which is the distance in between (a) and (b).

NORTH STREET *c.* 1730

on the other side of the street. The two cottages in the illustration give some idea of their architecture. Thomas Thompson's almshouses replaced some of these in 1618. Nearby to the south was a malthouse with a backside, orchard, and garden which the 9th Earl let in 1630 for twenty-one years to Sir William Goring, of Burton, Walter Bartlett, of Stopham, Henry Dawtrey, of Moore, William Mose junior, and ten other local gentry as a House of Correction for the Rape of Arundel. At the end of the term it was abandoned as a House of Correction and together with an adjoining property consisting of a tenement, barn, stable, and a parcel of waste was let to George Hampton for twenty-one years. In consideration of its ruinous condition, which he undertook to repair, he was allowed the first half-year's rent to buy timber. For the remaining 20½ years he was to pay £8 a year.

THE NORTH ENTRANCE TO PETWORTH IN 1791

The garden and temple on the right were, in 1610, part of the Coney Park, the wall being in the same place as the pale. Widow Howden's copyhold was outside the illustration to the right

A drawing by Samuel Grimm, by permission of the British Museum

NORTH STREET 1953

The cottages to the right were in North Street early in the seventeenth century. The wall on the left was built by the Duke of Somerset

MAP I

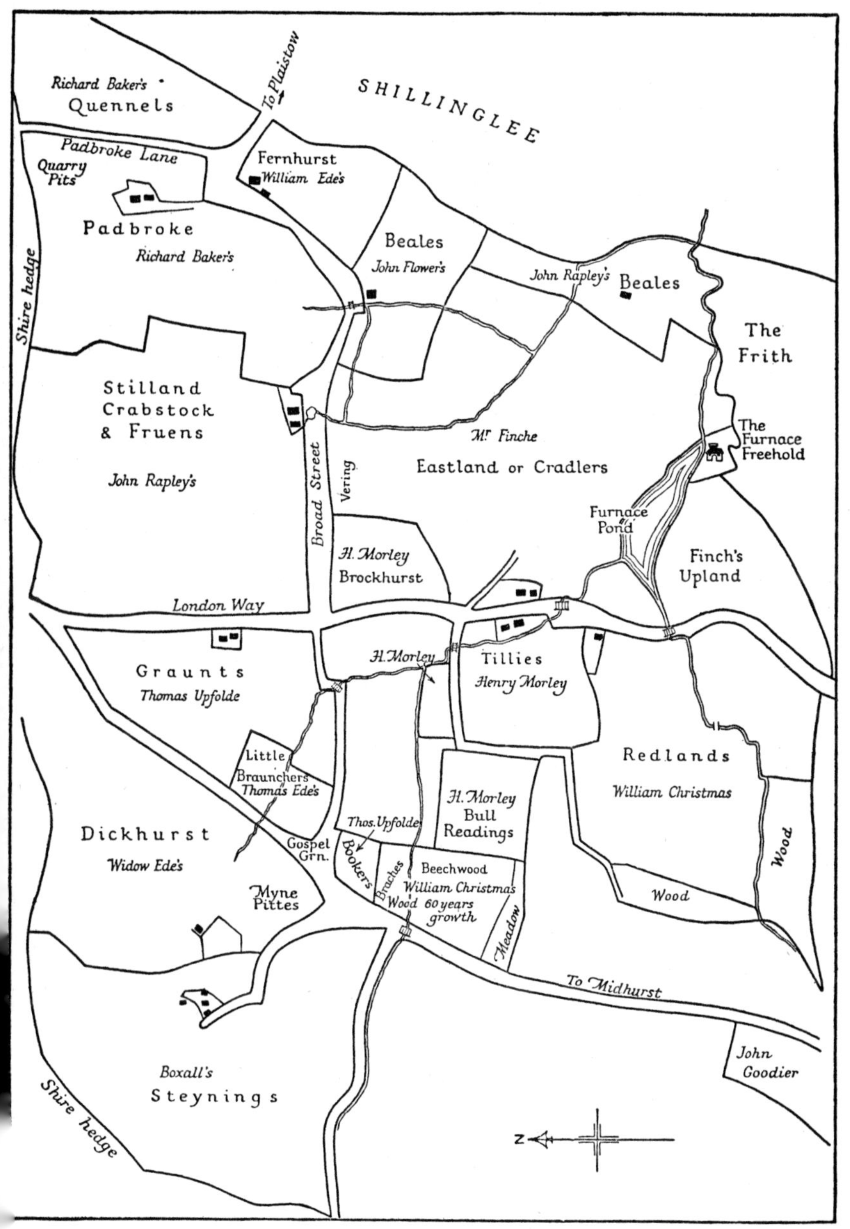

THE NORTHERN END OF THE MANOR

MAP II

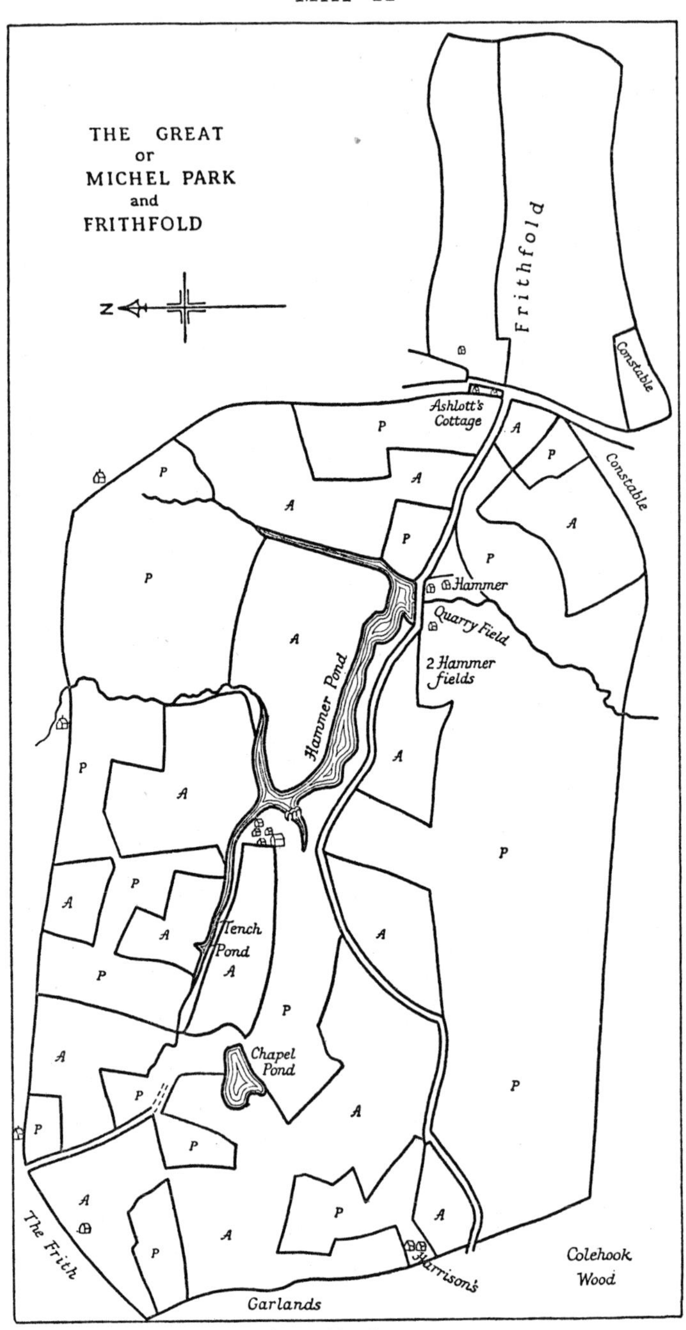

A=arable P=pasture

MAP III

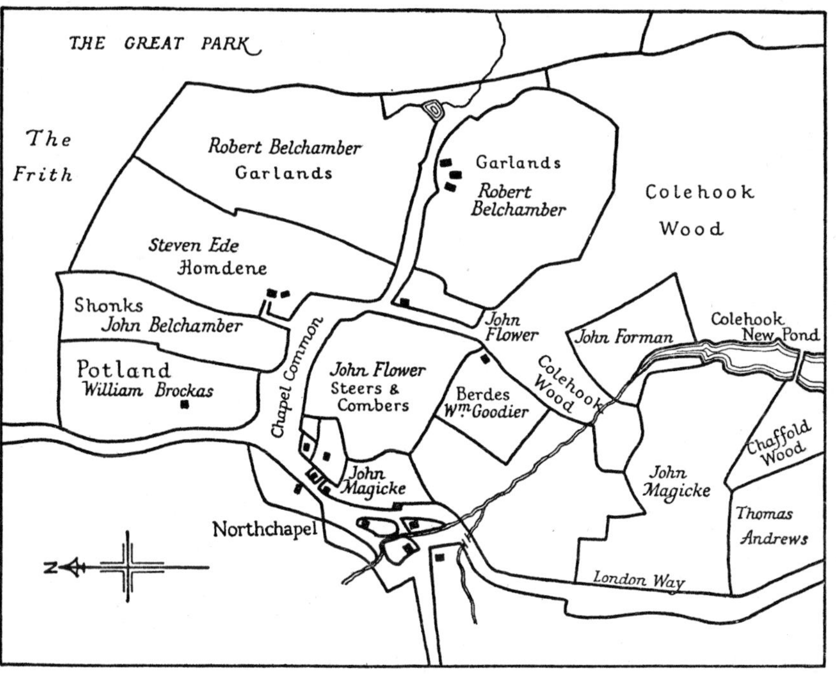

NORTHCHAPEL FARMS

MAP IV

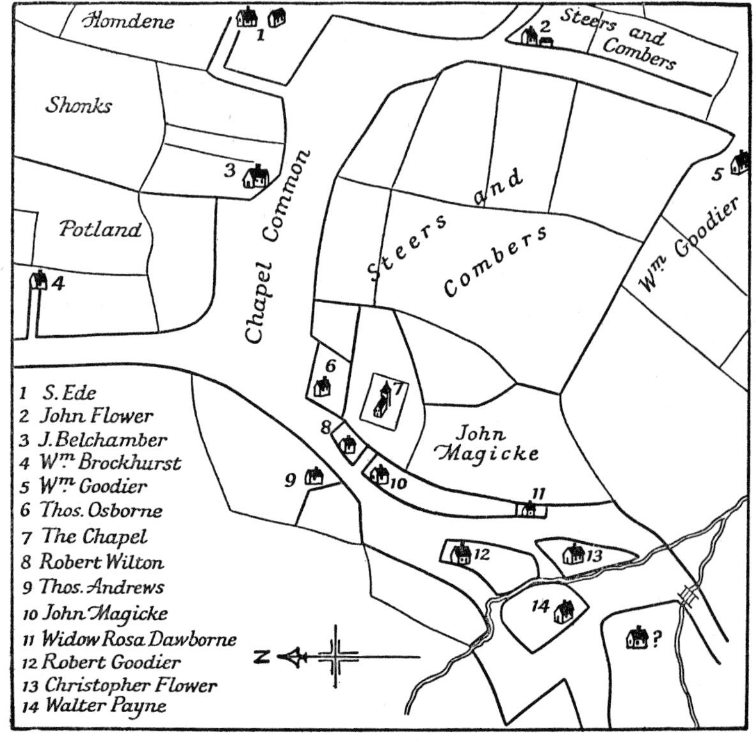
Homdene
Shonks
Potland
Chapel Common
Steers and Combers
Steers and Combers
Wm. Goodier
John Magicke
1 S. Ede
2 John Flower
3 J. Belchamber
4 Wm. Brockhurst
5 Wm. Goodier
6 Thos. Osborne
7 The Chapel
8 Robert Wilton
9 Thos. Andrews
10 John Magicke
11 Widow Rosa Dawborne
12 Robert Goodier
13 Christopher Flower
14 Walter Payne
N

NORTHCHAPEL VILLAGE

MAP V

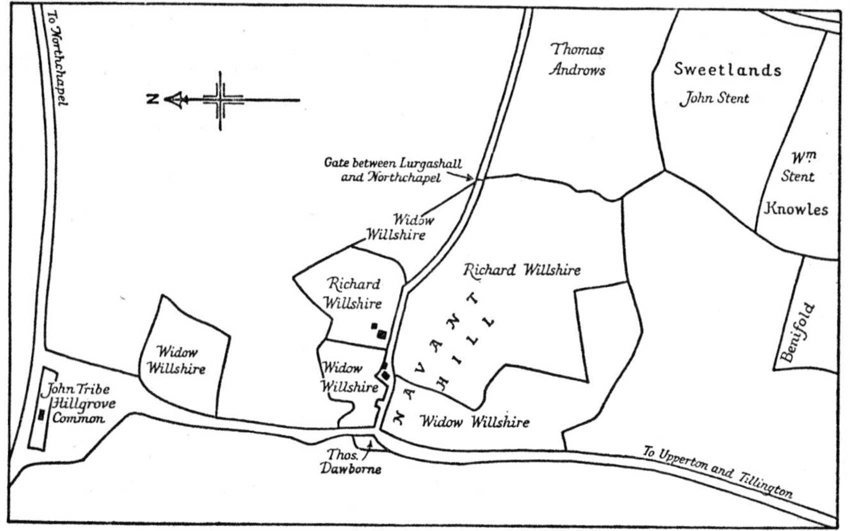

To Northchapel
N
Thomas Androws
Sweetlands
John Stent
Gate between Lurgashall and Northchapel
Wm Stent
Knowles
Widow Willshire
Richard Willshire
Richard Willshire
NAVANT HILL
Benifold
Widow Willshire
Widow Willshire
John Tribe Hillgrove Common
Widow Willshire
Thos. Dawborne
To Upperton and Tillington

NAVANT HILL

MAP VI

To Ebernoe
N
Streels Lane Gate
John Stent
William Coxe
Elkham
John Shude
Kechners
Edward Rawson
Sabins
Little London
John Stent
Colehook Mill
Robin Hood's Gdn
John Orton
MIDDLECARR
Colehook Old Pond
Colehook Wood
Knightleys
William Boyes
Laces
Widow Magicke
Ashfold
Brinckfold
John Shude
COMMON
Sweetlands
Widow Shertowe
Richard Boxall
Wisdoms
John Stent
New Pond
Chaffold Wood
Richard Boxall
Wisdoms
MIDDLECARR COMMON
Parks
John Stent
Wm Stent
Thomas Androws
John Stent
Sweetlands
Screech House
London Way
Copthurst Common
Park
Thomas Androws
Knowles
William Stent
Bishops
John Stent

COLEHOOK AND MIDDLECARR

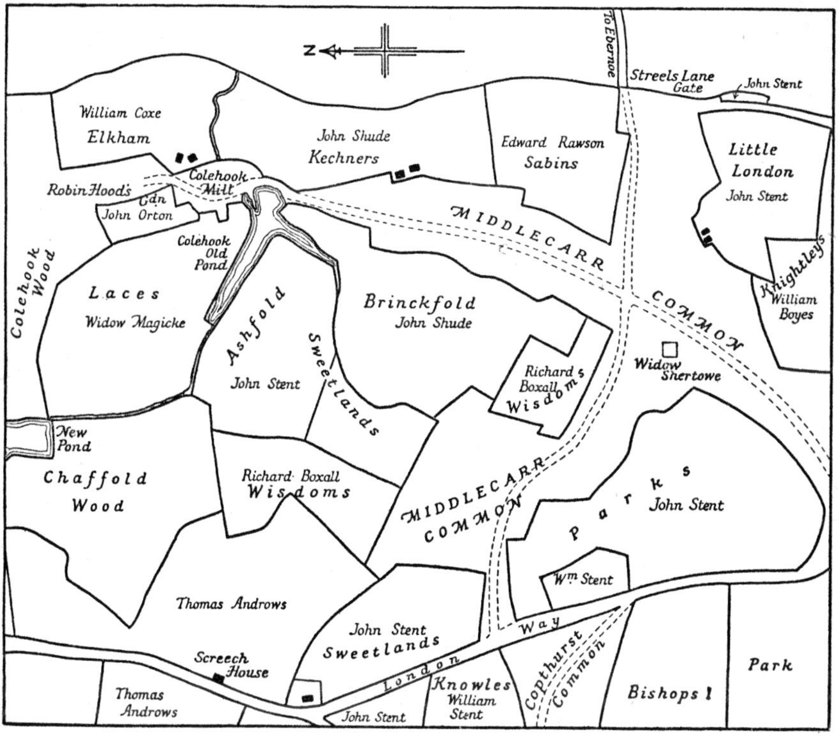

MAP VII

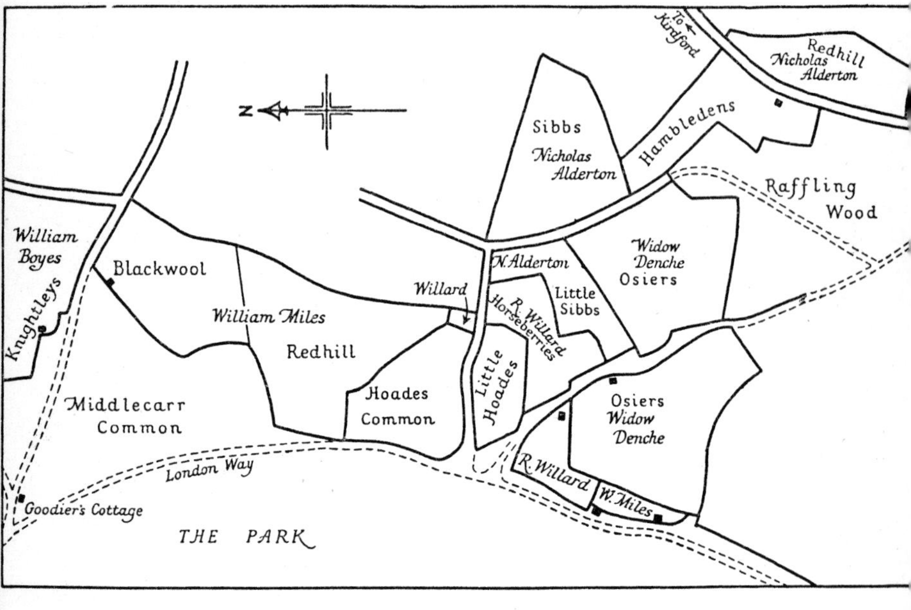

BLACKWOOL, SIBBS, AND OSIERS

MAP VIII

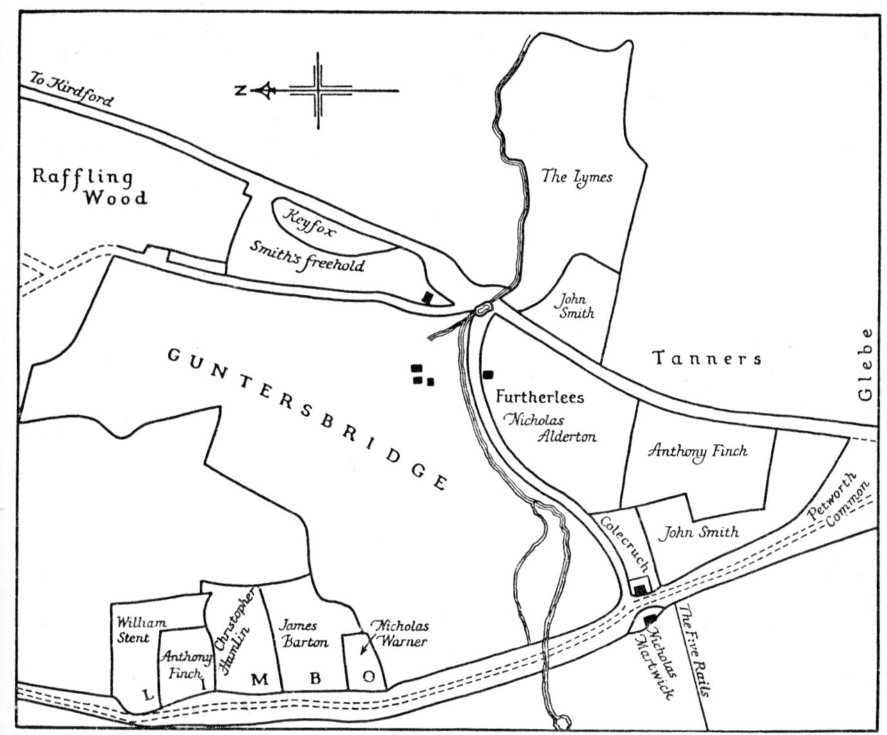

GUNTERSBRIDGE

MAP IX

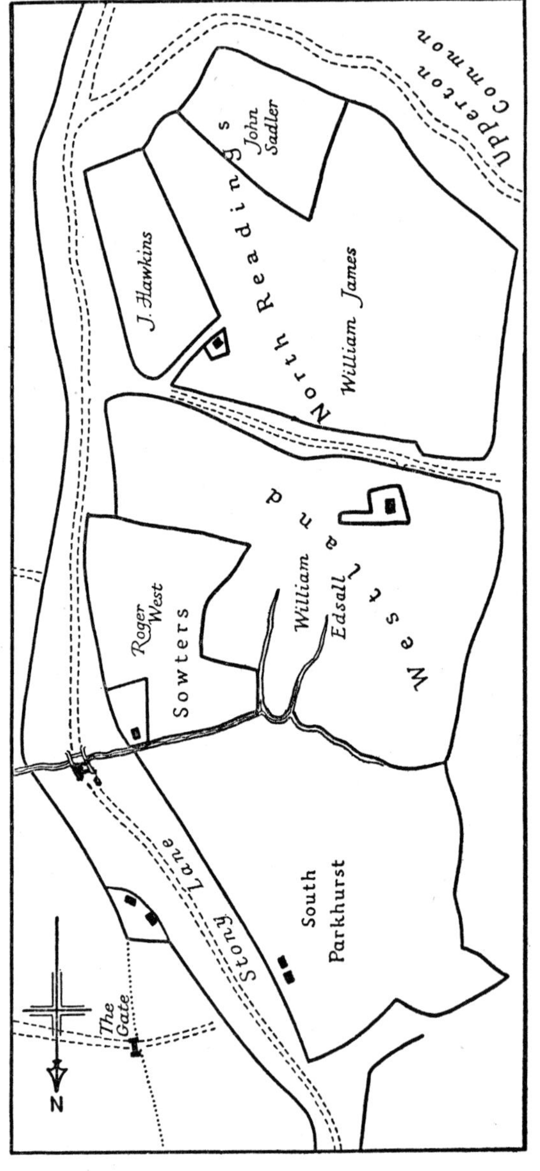

PARKHURST AND WESTLAND

MAP X

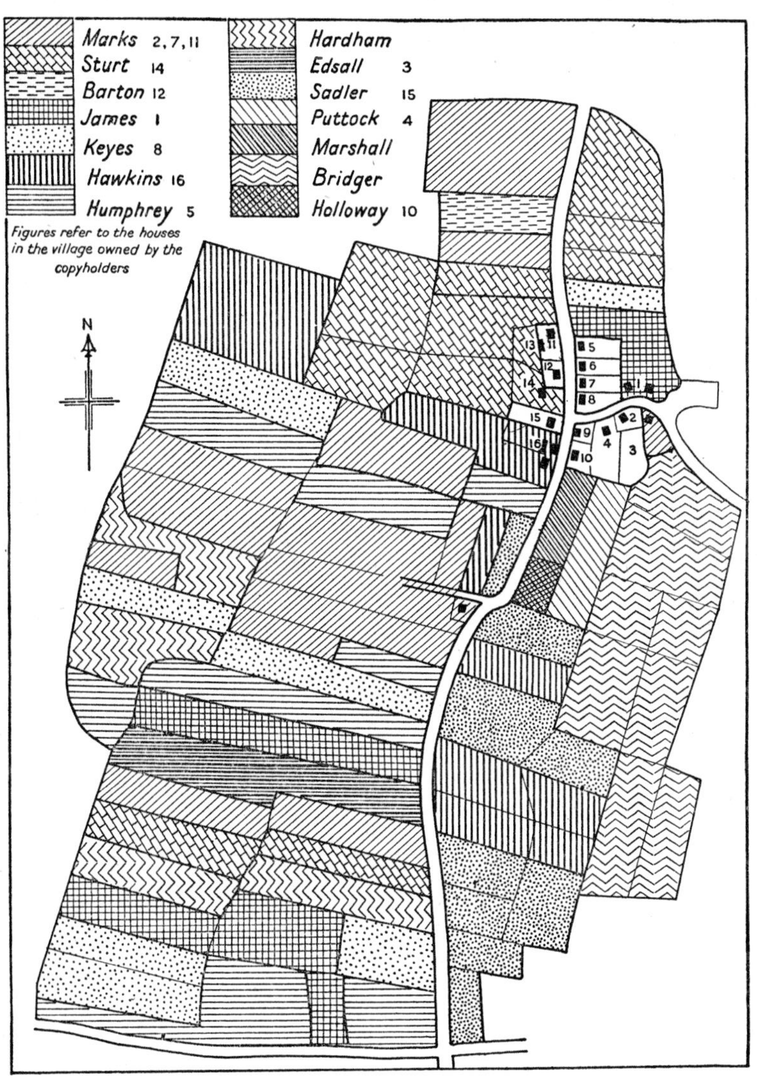
Marks 2,7,11
Sturt 14
Barton 12
James 1
Keyes 8
Hawkins 16
Humphrey 5
Hardham
Edsall 3
Sadler 15
Puttock 4
Marshall
Bridger
Holloway 10
Figures refer to the houses in the village owned by the copyholders
N
13
11
12
14
15
16
5
6
7
8
1
2
9
4
3
10

UPPERTON 1610

MAP XI

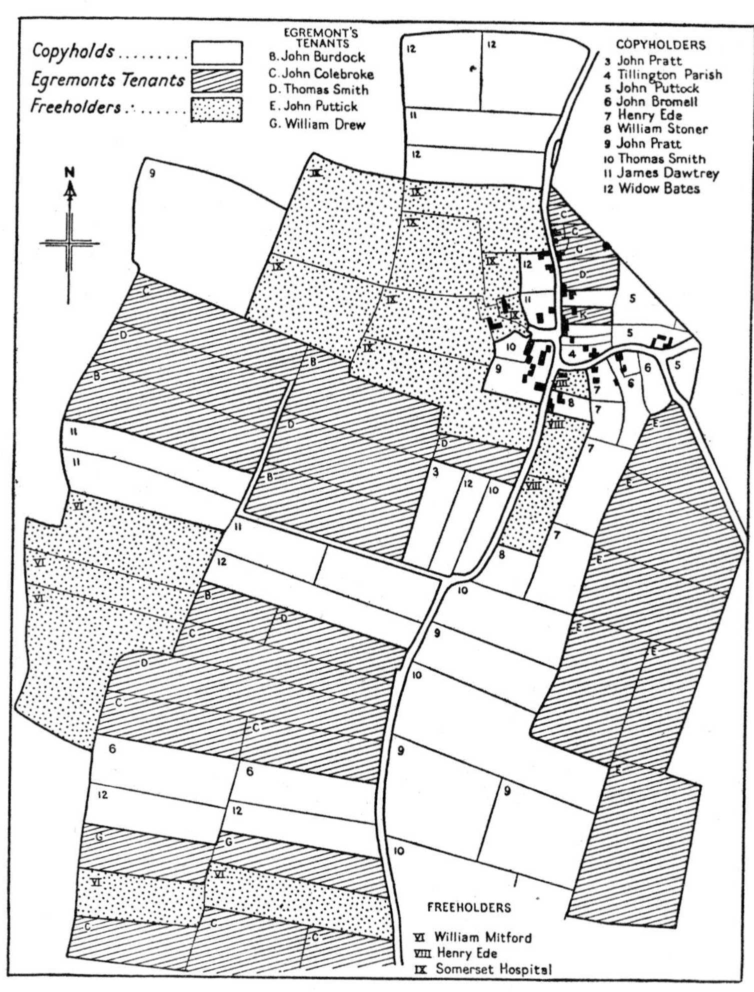

UPPERTON 1779

MAP XIII

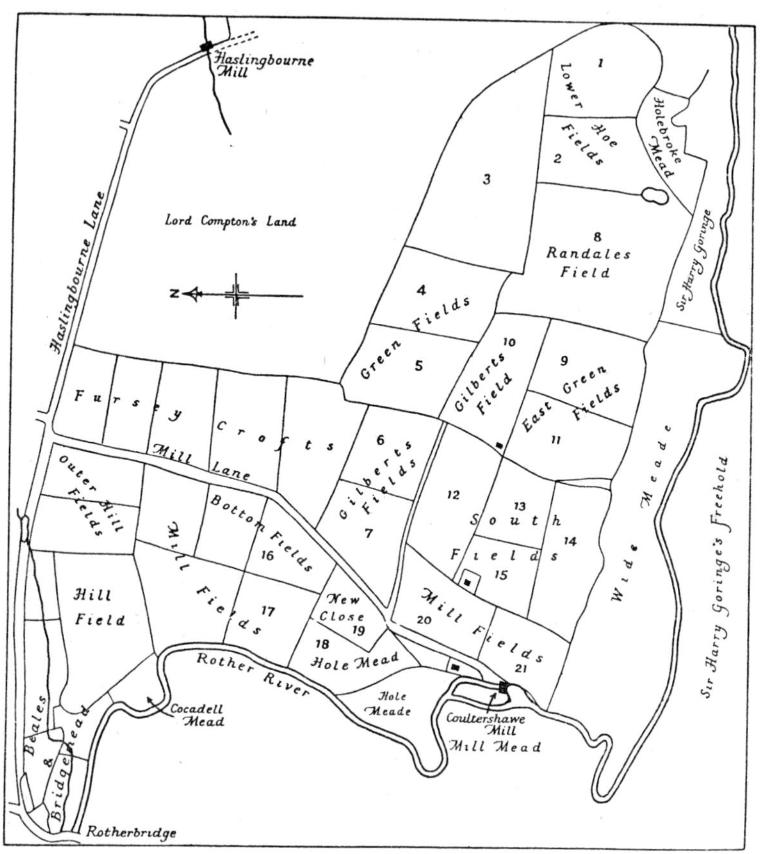

THE SOUTHERN END OF THE MANOR

MAP XIV

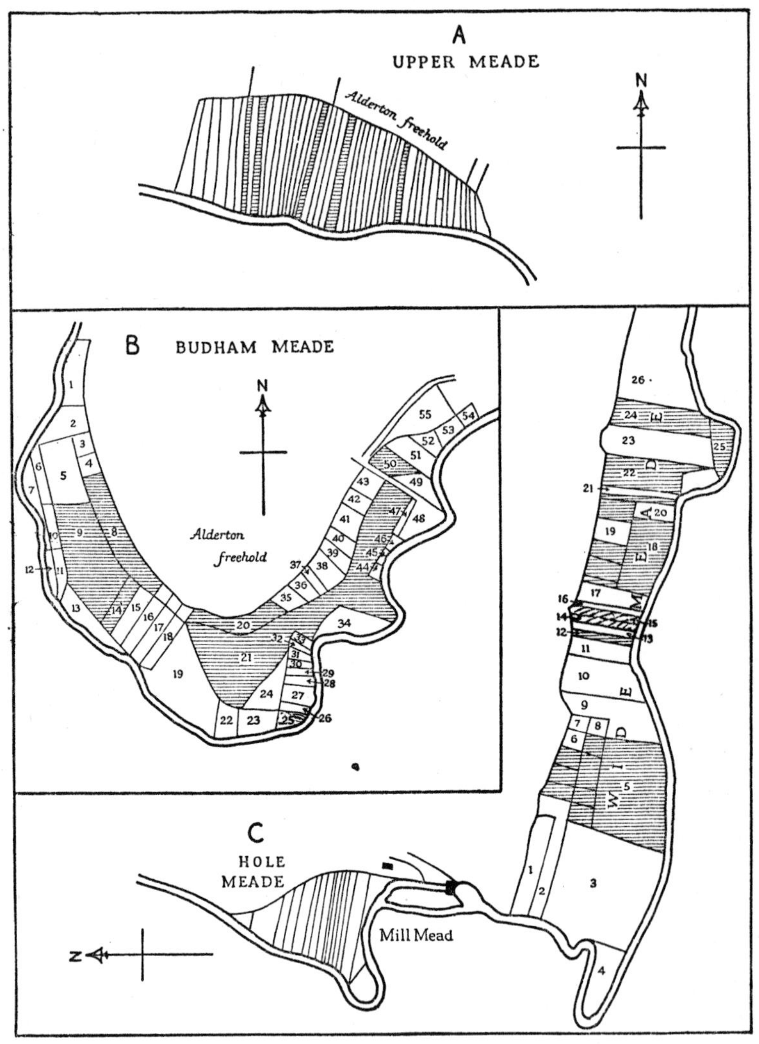

THE WATER MEADOWS

The shaded portions are so marked as being demesne
The names of other owners are illegible

XIVb. BUDHAM MEAD

1. Thomas Humphrey
2. Thomas Sturt
3. Apsley freehold
4. Dawtrey freehold
5. Mr. Cassies freehold
6. Apsley freehold
7. William Bridger
8. Demesne
9. Demesne
10. Glebe
11. Glebe
12. William Bridger
13. Elliot freehold
14. Demesne
15. John Sturt freehold
16. Padge freehold
17. Thomas Clowser(?)
18. William James
19. Alderton freehold
20. Demesne
21. Demesne
22. Sturt freehold
23. Richard Wilshire
24. Thomas Steyning freehold
25. Demesne
26. James(?)
27. (?) freehold
28. Thomson(?)
29. Ayer
30. Sturt
31. Thomson
32. Wimbold
33. (?)
34. Dawtrey freehold
35. Sturt
36. Aylwyne
37. Sturt
38. Thomson freehold
39. Aylwyne
40. Harding
41. Sturges
42. Aylwyne
43. Hamlin
44. Sturt
45. (?)
46. Sturt
47. Hamlin
48. Alderton
49. Sturt freehold
50. Demesne
51. Glebe
52. Dawtrey freehold
53. Peaton
54. Sturt
55. Alderton freehold

Demesne	7
Glebe	3
Freehold	16
Copyhold	29
	55

Not all these names are correct for 1610. For example, no. 34 was then John Smith's. Dawtrey was the previous owner.

XIVc. WIDE MEAD

1. Hayward (?)
2. (?) freehold
3. William Mose freehold
4. John Padge freehold
5. Demesne
6. R. Bowyer
7. John Sturt freehold
8. Ede
9. Dawtrey
10. Glebe
11. William Sturt
12. Demesne
13. Robert Willard
14. Demesne
15. Demesne
16. Widow Does
17. Dawtrey freehold
18. Demesne
19. (?) freehold
20. Smith freehold
21. (?) freehold
22. Demesne
23. Smith
24. Demesne
25. Demesne
26. Sir Henry Goring demesne of Byworth

MAP XVI

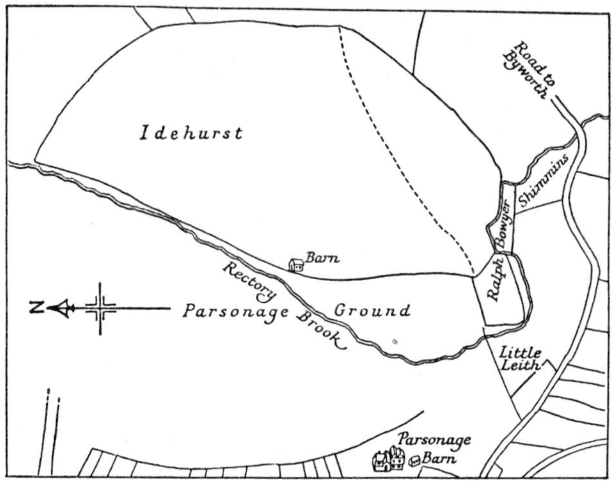

IDEHURST

MAP XVII

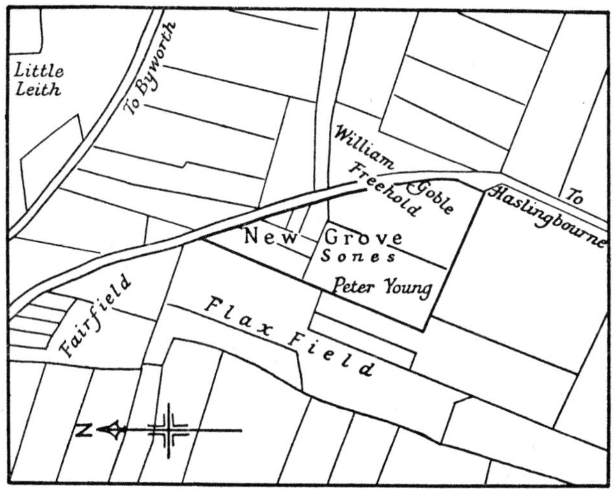

THE GROVE

MAP XVIII

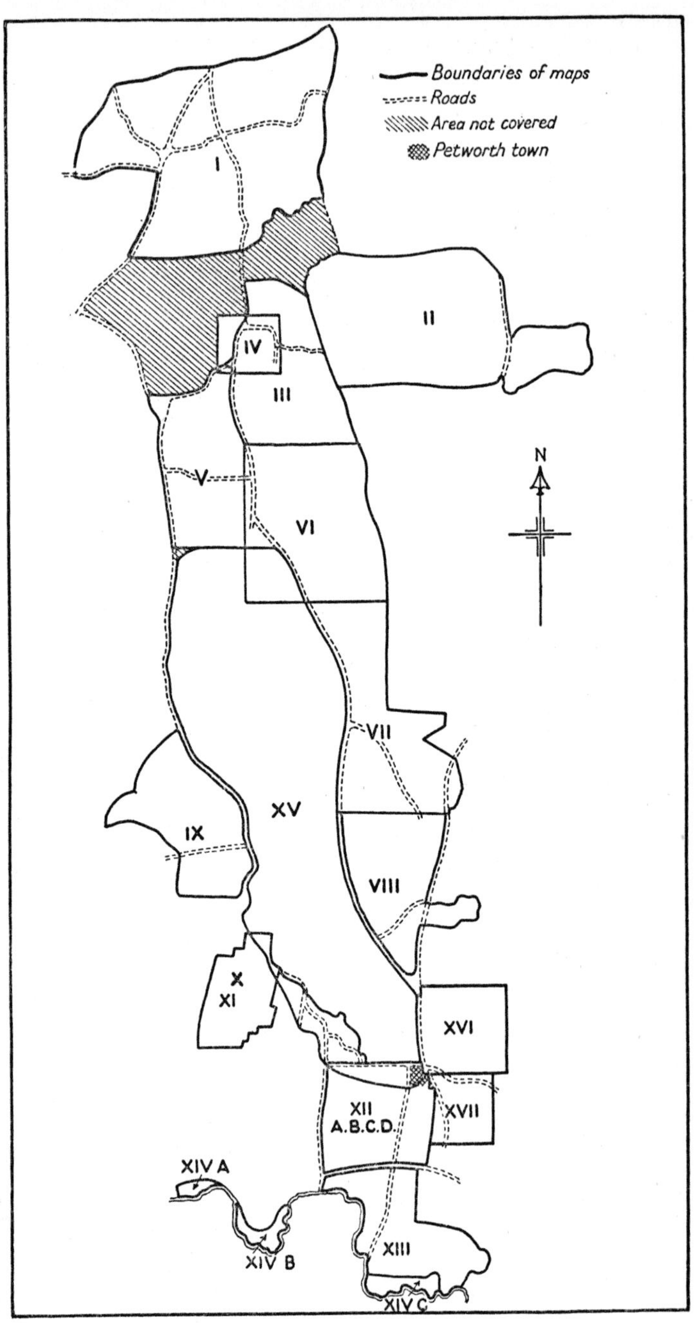

KEY-MAP

INDEX

Roman numerals in Index refer to maps in text

PRINTED IN
GREAT BRITAIN
AT THE
UNIVERSITY PRESS
OXFORD
BY
CHARLES BATEY
PRINTER
TO THE
UNIVERSITY